# "HELLO, HONEY, IT'S ME"

*The Story of Harry Chapin*

Ira Kantor

**Amazon KDP**

Copyright © 2020 Ira Kantor

All rights reserved.

No part of this book may be reproduced, or stored in a retrieval system, or transmitted in any form or by any means, electronic, mechanical, photocopying, recording, or otherwise, without express written permission of the publisher.

Cover and Book Photos: Courtesy of Chapin Productions LLC and HarryChapinMusic.com
Copyright Registration Number: TX 8-773-660
Printed in the United States of America

## *I WAS. I AM. AND NOW I WILL BE.*

*The life of Harry Chapin, charismatic musician and iconic humanitarian, was unexpectedly and tragically taken on July 16, 1981. He was 38 years old.*

*A "human dynamo" whose sheer tenacity landed him on the Billboard charts, on Broadway, in the White House, and at the forefront of the world hunger movement, Chapin lived by the mantra of "When in doubt, do something." In following this mentality, Chapin's 10-year solo career encompassed more than 2,000 concerts, nine studio albums, the creation of global nonprofit World Hunger Year (now WhyHunger), and the love and respect of fans, fellow musicians, and key political influencers alike.*

*Hailed as a consummate storyteller, Chapin is best known for his character-driven tunes — "Taxi," "Sniper," "W·O·L·D," "A Better Place to Be," "30,000 Pounds of Bananas," and "Cat's in the Cradle" included. Yet despite having only four Top 40 hits to his name, Chapin's songs remain one of a kind — elevating him to the same artistic status as classic singer-songwriters of his era like James Taylor, Jim Croce, Gordon Lightfoot, and John Denver.*

*Now, nearly 40 years after his death, the following 10-chapter oral biography seeks to tell Harry Chapin's story through the firsthand, on-the-record testimonies of the "characters" who knew him best — more than 65 family members, friends, business associates, and political and musical contemporaries. For context, Harry's own voice, along with other relevant news articles and reviews released during his lifetime, are included in italics.*

*While there are additional individuals and events that further shape Harry's tale, this book strives to provide a well-rounded retrospective of a musical shooting star whose life, being, sense of accomplishment, and legacy remain unsurpassed — even to this day.*

# CHAPTER 1

## *FALL IN LOVE WITH HIM*

**Rex Fowler (Musician, Aztec Two-Step):** Everyone loved Harry. If you met Harry, you just had to love the guy.

**Livingston Taylor (Musician):** I certainly was aware of Harry's career. I, like millions of other people, loved his storytelling.

**Janis Ian (Musician):** The world lost one of the kindest hearts in the music business when he died.

**Gordon Lightfoot (Musician):** He had a great personality and a wonderful talent to back it up. And the guts to carry it off.

**John Hall (Musician, Orleans):** He was a populist back when that word meant 'of the people, by the people, for the people.'

**Jackson Browne (Musician):** I actually don't think that (Harry) was quite nearly as well-known alive as when after he passed away with his commitment to ending world hunger. He was kind of here and then gone.

**Eric Andersen (Musician):** I appreciated his talent and

popularity. Like Jim Croce, he was far too young to leave this world.

**Ron Palmer (First guitarist):** Harry was a human dynamo. I mean if they could have hooked him up to electricity, he probably would have powered New York.

**Ken Kragen (Second manager):** This was one of the great human beings of our generation. And I must say that Harry Chapin was really one of the most unique individuals I've ever known—both in his dedication to his craft and humanity in general.

**Jaime Chapin Miller (Daughter):** Harry was committed to all things that came his way — parenting five kids; learning new things; lobbying Congress; making commitments to people and causes. He believed life was short and had to be lived every minute to the fullest.

**David Soul (Actor; Musician):** I knew Harry for a long time. You could say there was a mutual admiration on both sides, I think. He writes about real-life stories, which I really appreciate.

**John Davidson (Actor; Entertainer):** He was an incredibly talented, inspiring performer and writer.

**John Oates (Musician, Hall & Oates):** His songs had a universal appeal. He talked about universal topics but he brought them in a way that was very personal. I saw the way he could take some very, very large subjects and make them feel as though they were just a slice of everyday life. I felt he was really skilled and adept at that.

**Oscar Brand (Musician):** It was a very, very exciting business meeting Harry Chapin. Without question you could feel he was wrapped in electricity and excitement. He was a good, sweet man and there aren't that many.

By the way, in not only being sweet, and fine, and helpful, he was a great musician too. That's very important.

**Jason Chapin (Son):** A lot of people have a great life and they are famous for something, but they are soon forgotten. The fact that he's remembered by so many people and appreciated by so many people years after he's died is just sometimes very hard to believe.

**Ron Albert (Co-producer, *Sequel*):** The world is a better place because of Harry.

※ ※ ※

IRA KANTOR

# STORY OF A LIFE

**Harry Chapin (From a 1980 concert program):** *Arrived December 7, 1942, the obligatory first step to a life story. I become part of a large, exciting, sprawling, multifaceted brood. The second of my mother's six sons, followed by three more boys and three girls from my father's later marriages. A "rich little poor boy" childhood — with few creature comforts, but a family that provided all the love and stimulation I could absorb.*

*Childhood in New York City in the '40s — on West 11th Street by the Hudson River Piers. Lived in a three-room apartment above a longshoreman's office on a block halfway between the maximum security federal penitentiary and the M&M Trucking Company. But each summer, for three magical months, we escaped to Grandfather Burke's farm in New Jersey. No extra money was available in a family of artists, but still all the kingdoms of the mind were opened early — where every mental space was touched upon, except boredom.*

**Elspeth Hart (Mother):** My father was Kenneth Burke, and then James Chapin was a painter. He's quite well known as an American painter.

I knew Jim [Chapin] before he drummed. I was 14 and he was 15 and we had this house in the country in Andover, New Jersey. My father knew Jim Senior, and Jim Senior played tennis marvelously. Jim Senior came over out to our country place with this very tall, lanky boy.... So we met that way.

I think I had four children by the time I was 26.

**Bob Zachary (Former producer, Elektra Records):** Jim

Chapin ... invented a drum method way before guys like Joe Morello, who played with [Dave] Brubeck. It was basically learning how to play independents.

**Tom Chapin (Brother):** My dad was out of the family when I was three. Hugely important in our lives were the two grandmothers — Abby Chapin, who was my father's mother, and my mother's mother, Lily Burke.

Our lives early on were a big family thing during the year with our grandmothers who we would see several times a week, every week. Then we'd spend the whole summer in Andover, New Jersey with my grandmother at what was called "the compound" or "the farm" out there. As soon as school was out, we were there.

**Sandy Chapin (Wife):** Harry felt he had to earn respect in his own family and to find his position because there were assumptions that his brother James was the brain — uncontested position. His mother perceived that her firstborn was going to be another Kenneth Burke.

Harry was, from everything I've ever heard, the most delightful child. He was friendly. He was enthusiastic. Playful. Happy. Then there was Tom, and Tom was the all-American basketball player; the handsome athlete. And then there was Steve, and Steve played five instruments and was a musical genius.

**Tom Chapin:** When Harry was a kid he almost died several times because of his asthma, or at least we thought he would.

**Harry Chapin (From a 1980 concert program):** *The '50s brought changes.... A stepfather appeared on the scene and we moved to Brooklyn Heights.*

**Elspeth Hart:** The National Board of Review of Motion Pictures decided to get out a magazine called *Films in Review*. I was the editorial secretary.

My second husband, Henry Hart, who also was a writer and was much older and really was not a very good stepfather, had gone through a thing of being radical and then had seen the light and become — I don't know if reactionary is the word — but had gone back.

Considering I had four children in all this, I was really very naive. He was nice, and educated, and attractive, but we were just of such different backgrounds. He'd grown up in Philadelphia and he was a writer. He really couldn't deal with these four little boys.

Harry liked to have people approve of him when he was a child. He really liked to please people.

**Tom Chapin:** My father we'd see every weekend, but was very much not a father. More like a favorite uncle. He's not a father who's going to teach you how to whistle or go fishing with you. He was totally into his own world, but we adored him.

The four brothers got very, very tight. Then Henry Hart came into the picture and it was difficult for us and for him, I think. He was a mainline Philadelphia guy. Very interesting guy, but totally unequipped to take care of — and be the father of — four ruffian little guys. He was very much a stickler for manners. He was very proud of the fact that John Hart, his direct ancestor, had signed the Declaration of Independence.

He bought a brownstone in Brooklyn for $16,000 and we

moved to Brooklyn—45A Hicks Street. It was touchy for us, and Harry was the focal point of the touchiness. They just did not get along at all. No matter what Harry did, it was a problem. James, the oldest, would intellectually engage Henry and try to talk to him that way, but it was very hard for us all.

**Elspeth Hart:** My marriage was not very good, to put it mildly. And I had two new little boys by that time.

**Harry Chapin (From an unedited typing exercise, February 1964):** *Every morning (Henry's) alarm would ring at exactly 7 o'clock (for he was a very exact man) and he would call up: 'Is everybody up' and everybody would shout back in turn, 'Yes Father,' 'Yes Father,' 'Yes Father,' 'Yes Father' (there were 4* [sic] *of us). At seven-fifteen* [sic] *we were all supposed to have our beds made and be dressed, and then we would start on cleaning our rooms. He would call up and ask if all of the beds were made (we were on the top floor and he only came up once and* [sic] *a while to see if things were going as he wished. When they weren't, there was hell to pay for he usually batted around somebody until he felt that they had payed* [sic] *for their errors). And then by 7 thirty* [sic] *we were supposed to have cleaned our rooms and be downstairs helping mother with the breakfast. At 7:45 he came downstairs and we all ate breakfast, and left for school at 8 A M* [sic] *sharp.*

**Tom Chapin:** Dinner would start out fairly mellow and then he'd have a full decanter of wine. By the end, he'd be angry at somebody. Usually Harry.

Henry found a can opener that had been bent and [said] 'Who did it.' Sort of like the strawberries in *The Caine Mutiny*, you know. It was like: 'Nobody's going to do anything until you tell me who broke this can opener.'

To this day, we don't know how it happened. It was so ludicrous.

Every time it was a Harry birthday, especially when he was a teenager — December 7 — there would always be a war. One year — I think it was when he turned 17 — Henry kicked him out of the house. (Harry) walked from Brooklyn over the Brooklyn Bridge ... to the Village and knocked on the door of my mother's sister.

My mother always says, to this day, that was the worst day of her life. She says, 'I should have just walked then.' But she had two little boys, Jeb and John. That was a messy, messy awful thing.

The thing about our upbringing [was] there was this incredible other side of people who would welcome you in a heartbeat.

**Elspeth Hart:** We moved out one day without saying we were moving out. Henry came home and we weren't there.

* * *

## *THERE ONLY WAS ONE CHOICE*

**Harry Chapin (From a 1980 concert program):** *I joined the Grace Church Choir with younger brothers Tom and Steve, and started taking trumpet lessons. The summer of '57 brought two gigantic discoveries, girls and guitars. At my cousin's barn a copy of* The Weavers at Carnegie Hall *played constantly, and the trumpet lessons faded away. I find* *an old banjo in the attic and start playing. Tom buys a guitar, and Steve starts playing four string tenor guitar, tipple, and a stand-up bass. Folk music, the ultimate social weapon, becomes my full-time passion.*

**Tom Chapin:** My Grandma Chapin — Abby Chapin — really wanted us to know the language of music. When we were in the Village, we started going to Greenwich House Music School on Barrow Street. Harry took trumpet. I took clarinet under duress and Steve and James both took piano. We learned how to read music.

**Harry Chapin (From *The Tonight Show Starring Johnny Carson* – August 10, 1977):** *I played classical trumpet until I was about 15. Then I found out girls like guitar players better and quickly shifted over.*

**Elspeth Hart:** (Harry's) trumpet playing was a little wild.

**Diana Chapin (Sister-in-law):** All of the boys probably had musical talent. My husband [Jim], when he was very young, lost his hearing. He had about 90 percent loss in one ear and about 40 percent in the other. It was the result of a childhood illness. They didn't realize initially what was wrong; that he had a really serious ear infection. Harry got something similar a few years later. Then they knew what it was, so they were able to catch it in time.

**Tom Chapin:** When we moved to Brooklyn, I went to P.S. 8. We were half a block from the school. In the early fall of that first year — I guess I'm 8 years old — one of my classmates said, 'I'm going to try out for a boys choir at Grace Church.' I made the mistake of telling my mom that he was going to do that, and she got very interested. She found out when (the audition) was and made the phone calls.

That Thursday I got dragged the length of Brooklyn Heights. All the way I'm going, 'No, I don't want to. No!' And she's grabbing me: 'Yes you are.'

**Big John Wallace (Bassist):** Grace Church in Brooklyn Heights was one of the great choirs, at least in Brooklyn. I mean you actually got paid.

The choir director, Anne Versteeg McKittrick, was an amazing woman. She had just as much of an effect on all of us as our parents did. Maybe even more in certain circumstances. A total authority figure and she was just great. Ran the thing with an iron fist. All the little kids were scared to death of her because she could be tough, but it was a great experience. I kid around about it on stage now, but my career, in a sense, did peak when I was 12. I was the soprano soloist in the choir and that was really cool.

Harry was never in the choir. Tom is two years younger than I am. Steve is three years younger. So that's a big age difference when you're nine or 10. I think I came in in '52 and Steve came in about three years later — '55 — so that's when we met. I mean we could play around or whatever, but that was a big age gap then. I didn't really get friendly or really close to Steve until much later. It was after they went to college and all. Anyway, we got a great musical education there.

**Tom Chapin:** Also in that choir was Bobby Lamm — Robert Lamm — who would be the lead singer for Chicago.

We were all involved until we went into college. All the

way through because once your voice changed you became an alto. So it went from 1953 until I went away to college in '62, so that's what — nine years. Steve was there longer — two more years.

The music thing, we were steeped in it and also you'd see your dad play every once in a while. He'd come into our lives and you'd see him at a jazz place. Here's this beautiful man having a great time behind the drums. Took it totally seriously but also just loving it. So it was kind of an example of a guy who had the most fun in the entire world playing music and dressed to the nines — as you did in the Big Band era — and just enjoying it. I can't tell you how important that was for us.

**Harry Chapin (From a 1980 concert program):** *In 1958, The Chapin Brothers, singing three-part pubescent harmony, go public for the first time. Reaction is generous enough to sink the hook in deeper. Soon there are $20 gigs at neighborhood parties, band breaks, and society dances. The Chapin Brothers become junior folkies, on the periphery of the Greenwich Village hotbed of an exploding folk boom.*

**Tom Chapin:** Grandma Chapin had an old Stuart banjo in her basement that had been her brother's. Harry got it fixed up and got the Pete Seeger book and began to play. I got my first guitar — a plywood Kay guitar, I think — for 50 bucks or something. And we started learning Weavers songs. Then we talked Steve into playing with us. So we had a trio and, of course, what was really cool about this [is] Harry was the lead dog, the older brother, but Steve and I — because we're choir boys — we could sing harmony. Harry was usually the melody guy; Steve and I would do various harmonies. For the next 10, 12 years that was our hobby. We got more and more professional and eventually started playing in the Village and stuff. But it was very much like, 'Hey we can do this together.'

We had a stepfather who we really hated, but we had this other incredibly valuable creative physical clan. The music really was an outgrowth of this incredible artistic family clan. That's where it started.

**Stefan Grossman (Musician):** At that age, we were fantastically interested in learning everything we could. It was the beginning of the folk revival for our age which would have been The Kingston Trio. Then it would have been Joan Baez and Oscar Brand.

We were schoolmates at Brooklyn Tech and I was learning guitar with Reverend [Gary] Davis at that time. Tom was playing guitar and banjo as well. We'd get together to just play. The culmination is we all performed — me, Tom, Harry, and Steve; the three Chapin brothers, sort of like a Kingston Trio type of unit. We did a performance in Brooklyn Tech. That's when I really got to know Harry and the Chapin brothers. They were all great singers and they could all sing harmonies fantastically well.

**Tom Chapin:** We took the test for Brooklyn Tech because we were Brooklyn boys. The first four brothers all made it.

**Oscar Brand:** They were all musicians, that whole damn family. They knew where the excitement should be and where they would entice the audience into listening and splash it on them like hot tea.

**Tom Chapin:** Another connection was that around the corner from us in Brooklyn Heights lived Earl Robinson. I mean we're doing folk music; we didn't know who he was. His son, Jimmy Robinson, is a great friend of Steve's and they're getting in great trouble in the Heights, you know. They're hanging out.

Living downstairs [from] Earl Robinson at that time was Lee Hays. Now we never connected it but Lee Hays was the bass singer in The Weavers, and he had a leather couch. Harry was doing leatherwork at that point. So Jimmy told Earl that Harry was doing leather stuff. Harry goes over … and fixes Lee Hays' couch. We didn't know who Lee Hays was until later on I go, 'Oh!' It's interesting because we were trying to do folk music and then we didn't even connect with what was around.

**Diana Chapin:** Harry would always be leading the pack. It was like a joke that he would be way ahead of everybody else physically. He'd start off and if you were all in a group he'd be way ahead. Harry was very enthusiastic. (Jim) used to say, 'Chill down, Harry,' because he'd get so over the top enthused about things. It was his nature.

# OLD COLLEGE AVENUE

**Harry Chapin (From a 1980 concert program):** *In 1960, high school is over, and in the next three years I manage to spend three months in the Air Force Academy before resigning; three terms at Cornell before busting out.*

**Gary Howe (Vice president, United States Air Force Academy Association of Graduates):** Harry Chapin would have been in the Class of 1964. He was here at the Academy as a cadet from 27 June 1960 to sometime in August 1960, which means that he would have been here for what we call Basic Cadet Training and left at the end of that.

**Elspeth Hart:** (Harry) went to the Air Force Academy. The hazing was absolutely horrible. He couldn't stand it. Here he was, one of four boys with his grandmothers and me teaching, 'You don't tease people. You get along.' Then he went to this place and I think he didn't eat for three days.

**Tom Chapin:** I think he went to the Air Force Academy because Henry wanted him to go. Nobody else did. It was a nutty idea, but Henry talked to a congressman who got him in.

**Harry Chapin (From an unedited typing exercise, February 1964):** *The only other time (in) my life, besides those five years with my stepfather, that I lived any kind of regemented [sic] existence was at my brief stint in the Air Force*

*Academy.*

**Glenn Coleman (Cadet, United States Air Force Academy Class of 1964):** Your first day there is really scary because you go from being a high school hot dog to really a number where they shave your head and put you in a uniform. There's just a lot of screaming that goes on for the whole summer. Every moment that you're there, there's somebody in your face except at night. In other words, when you go to bed at night you're guaranteed eight hours and that's pretty much the only time you have to yourself.

**Dave Neal (Cadet, United States Air Force Academy Class of 1964):** We were in the 42nd Cadet Training Squadron. There were probably 30 to 40 classmates in that squadron and then the upperclassmen were in charge of the hazing. We had to march at attention at all times everywhere. At meals we sat on the front three inches of our chair and looked only down at our plate unless we were addressed by an upperclassman who was giving us more attention in meals than we wanted.

**Glenn Coleman:** You're going to take one week out of that in the last half and you go to the mountains for survival. In that case, you're living up there for a week. Basically, it's Boy Scout camp. In other words, you're out there learning how to skin a rabbit; learning how to find food; learning how to trap an animal; learning how to fish — just learning how to survive out in the wilderness. Even though it's not highly technical as far as they are not really creating "Crocodile Dundee" out there; it's a confidence builder that they are teaching you how to survive.

**Dave Neal:** A lot of push-ups. A lot of push-ups. All the time, lots of push-ups. Anytime an upperclassman looked at you, it was like, 'Hit it for 10!' or 'Hit it for 20!' I remember a couple of evenings or maybe weekends when we had a few minutes to do something on our own that some of us would gather in Harry's room and he'd break out his guitar and play and sing.

**Elspeth Hart:** A dean or somebody at the Air Force, in trying to make him stay there, said, 'If you don't succeed in this, you'll never succeed in anything else.'

**Harry Chapin (From *The Tonight Show Starring Johnny Carson* – August 10, 1977):** *Actually, I have sort of a mixed academic history because I busted out of Cornell University twice, once in architecture and once ... in philosophy. It means that not only could I not build a library; I wouldn't know what to inscribe around it.*

**Diana Chapin:** Harry flunked out of Cornell at some point and he had gone to the Air Force Academy prior to that for a while. Jim felt badly because, at one point, he was ... writing these sorts of letters to Harry and he felt he wasn't supportive enough at the time. Looking back on it he said, 'Geez, he was having a hard time and I should have been more supportive.'

**Harry Chapin (From a 1980 concert program):** *By the end of '63, I am in love and thinking I should give one more shot at finishing college. But my second attempt at Cornell, and my first attempt at a love affair follow the same pattern — pyrotechnic beginnings followed by gradual decline. Ironically this educational and emotional merry-go-round makes a fertile climate for my first songs. They fall into the usual categories for young prophets: protest songs and lugubrious ballads of unrequited love. It takes four terms to bust out this* *time.*

**James Maas (Former professor, Cornell University):** I met Harry when he was an undergraduate student at Cornell and was taking a psychology course from me. That course had small discussion sessions, as well as a large lecture.

On several occasions, Harry came up to me after lecture and said, 'I'm in a quandry, I don't know what to do. I'm struggling with the curriculum in architecture and one of the reasons I'm struggling is because I have always wanted to be a folk singer. Yet I know it's nearly impossible to make a living doing that. I think my dad would like me to get some applied degree so I can make some money, but my heart is really in folk singing. I just don't want to disappoint my father. On the other hand, I feel that I'm leaving something that I'd like to go with.'

I said, 'Harry, you're always going to regret not trying, and so you absolutely have to devote a couple of years to singing and see how it goes. You can always come back and be in architecture and get further education. But now is your time. Follow what's in your heart. If you're good, you're going to be successful. If you're not good, at least somebody will tell you you're not going to make it and then you can have that to make further decisions.'

We had that conversation, I'd say, three or four or maybe five times.

**Harry Chapin (From an unedited typing exercise, February 1964):** *When I was in Architecture school at Cornell I always used to come up with projects at the last moment. Surprisingly enough about half of them weren't bad. They called* *them Chapin's one-day Wonders, or Oneders. The other half got chops, which is architecture lingo for failing, which is the reason I am not there today, partially. They called these chop projects Chapin's one-day Wonders too!*

**Tom Chapin:** Harry, when he was at Cornell, got involved with The Sherwoods, who were sort of like The Whiffenpoofs. They're Cornell's a cappella group. He was always trying to be in that group, but ... he was not equipped for it. But Fred Kewley, who was the head of it, became a really good friend and Harry's first manager.

**Fred Kewley (First manager):** It was 1961 and as freshmen at Cornell we both were intrigued with this a cappella singing group called The Sherwoods. We both tried out and, against all odds, we both got in. (Harry) was with us maybe two months or something and then he bounced out of school. He just wasn't doing well with school. Over the years, he came back to Cornell and studied architecture and bounced out; came back and studied something else and bounced out. He never did finish.

He's the first guy I had ever known personally that could play guitar and actually put a song across playing guitar. This is back in '62, '63. This is coming off the folk days with The Kingston Trio ... so to be able to do that was very impressive. Even back then in those college days, he would lean over that guitar and stare you right in the face and just completely sell you on whatever song he was singing at the time. He was always a super salesman when it came to most everything, but especially in putting his songs across and making the listener just get into it. He wasn't background music in any way.

I lived with Harry, Tom, Steve, and James and their

mother. I think it was a two bedroom, one living room, one kitchen apartment in Brooklyn Heights for like three months. They are all loud. Steve used to say about Harry: 'Two is company and Harry is a crowd.'

**Harry Chapin (From an unedited typing exercise, February 1964):** *Yes, my academic career has been rather mixed, an odd assortment, but except for brief flashes of brilliance, rather on the negative achievement side. My two stints at Cornell were the culmination of this.*

❈ ❈ ❈

**Harry Chapin (From an unedited typing exercise, February 1964):** *Yeah, I sing with my next two younger brothers, and we are going to make a million dollars, or so we think...*

**Harry Chapin (From a 1980 concert program):** *By 1965 I'm beginning to realize that I am not going to progress through life following the normal patterns. My brothers and I decide to get serious about our music. All the guitar playing that has been a crutch to our social lives, that has made us a couple of bucks on the side, that has given us something to do besides drinking beer on street corners, now is put to the test. We resolve to become full-time professionals. It's a summer of airborn [sic] dreams, potentials and performances, and yes, it felt like somehow, somewhere, sometime we were going to make it.*

*Dad joined the group that summer and backed us up on drums. We were still green but we were definitely different: part folk, part rock, topped with Grace Church harmonies and a jazz beat from the old man swinging in behind. But in September, Vietnam forces Tom and Steve back to college, and I'm back at square one.*

**Tom Chapin:** Dad was recording for Music Minus One. He knew [owner] Irv Kratka, and that summer Irv Kratka came and saw us play. He offered us studio time, but basically it was like Dad was playing with us. Also at that point [drummer] Phil Forbes was playing as well, and he was more of a rock drummer. He's on the record [*Chapin Music!*] too.

In like three days we went in and recorded 12 songs, 14 songs, whatever is on the record. It was kind of a blur. We just get in front of a microphone and just bash away and sing it and then, 'OK, that's that one. Let's do the next one.' It was basically what we were doing live and then we overdubbed something.

Here's an interesting story you may or may not have heard. September or maybe early October of my junior year, I believe, The Chapin Brothers are going to play at Hawkins Hall. We sold out Hawkins Hall, which is 600 people at the Hall in Plattsburgh. It's one of those things where everybody came and they're all saying, 'Geez I hope this is good; it's Tommy.' We get out there and start that first number; it was called "Walk Tall." And then Dad comes out on the drums towards the end. We ended it and — a standing ovation.

That happened on Saturday night. On Monday we were supposed to try out for a new TV show called *The Monkees* in New York City. We're driving home and Dad has this Studebaker with his drums up on the roof. In the back it's full of our guitars. Steve is taking the bus. Dad's driving and Dad very often had tires that were like threadbare. After we get down to Albany — Harry's got his learner's permit — Dad says, 'I'm getting tired, do you want to drive?' He says, 'Sure.' He gets behind the wheel and we're near Cairo, New York on the thruway; cars all around us and a bus behind us. We're going about 60, 65 miles per hour on the thruway — right rear tire blows and Harry's driving. I'm asleep ... across the back seat — this is before seat belts, you know — and Dad's in the suicide seat. It goes 'BOOM! DU DU DU DU!' and Dad says, 'Don't try to steer out of it.' Harry turns and the car rolls once off the road, twice — I'm holding on with my feet against the roof — three times. Comes to a halt.... My dad reaches over and turns off the thing. I start kicking the door to get out. Harry has broken the steering wheel with his jaw. And my father — the whole thing kind of caved in on his head. It turned out later his neck was broken but he didn't know.

What saved us was the drums on the top.

Dad, when he was a kid, fell out of a tree and his top three vertebrae in his neck are fused from that. So they take an X-ray of his neck; it looks like a normal neck. What actually happened was he broke all of the fuses left there and for the next month he's in terrible agony. It's funny, his mother sent him to a specialist and he has to wear one of those braces around his neck.

We go in to try out for *The Monkees* and Steve's there. We open up the guitars and the back of (Harry's) Martin was totally busted. We hadn't even looked at it. So we sang our stuff. They're kind of interested in me but not the band. That's as far as it went.

In another life I might have been Peter Tork.

**Fred Kewley:** Tom Chapin called me out of the blue one day. He had a group called The Chapins. They had gotten a deal with Epic Records. But Epic didn't seem to even know they existed and their manager at the time wasn't getting anything done. So Tom called me and said, 'Do you want to manage us?' I mean out of the blue. It's probably one of the smarter things I had done up to that point.

THE CHAPIN BROTHERS

# CHAPTER 2

## *SANDY*

**Sandy Chapin (Wife):** In the very beginning when I first met Harry, I kind of thought of it as a stepladder or a stairway. I felt as though I were moved to use my mind. He had such a lively, investigating energetic mind and I felt that it made me try to push; to think more or to reach. It was very exciting. I really think that that was the big dynamic from the beginning. I always said I married his mind.

**Jen Chapin (Daughter):** I remember very vividly it was very powerful. They met really out of sheer love. They met through him giving her guitar lessons. She objects to a lot of the details of "I Wanna Learn a Love Song," but she said they did just talk about poetry. And she said, 'I was done with my marriage when our relationship started.' There was no overlap.

**Sandy Chapin:** The story of meeting Harry is longer than it would seem because I was raising three children. I was very interested in doing a lot of arts and crafts at home, and painting, and then also going around the city to cultural experiences. The one thing that was missing was music. I'm not musical. As an elementary [school] teacher, I had to learn to teach music. One of the things I learned [was] that one of the uniquely American kinds of music are folk songs. I thought it would be really great to be able to share those with the kids as they were growing up. I had taken piano lessons for five years and although I could pick out songs on the piano, it was a different kind of thing with kids because I would be sitting there with my back to them, theoretically. The whole picture just didn't fit. So I decided I should learn to play guitar.

It might have been 1967. I had a friend in Brooklyn Heights where we lived who worked with organizations like the Brooklyn Academy of Music. I asked her to recommend a guitar teacher. She recommended Harry — the two families were neighbors and friends in Brooklyn Heights. I called the number and his mom answered and said that he was working in California and would probably be out there for a while. That was the end of that. I guess I tried a couple of other suggestions. I remember I got the name of somebody who was in Upper Manhattan and I thought, 'Well this doesn't make sense because I'd have to pay to get a babysitter in order to take the subway for an hour to go uptown to take a guitar lesson.' So I kind of dropped the whole thing.

Then one day, out of the blue, I got a call from Harry who had finished his work in California. His mother thought that he ought to get out of the house and get busy, so she gave him the telephone number that I guess she had pinned to the wall. He called. At this point it was really a surprise.

One of the things that was interesting was right away he said something to the effect that, 'When I'm teaching, I'm really serious about it and if you're not serious, it's not going to work out.' So, as I say, not having any musical inclination, I thought that I better work real hard.

He was skinny. He was very lean and clean-shaven. He would come in and whatever the length of the lesson was supposed to be — maybe it was 40 minutes or whatever — he said, 'I want to play you a song that I've just written.' Probably he had a collection of songs, and so he would sit there and perform. He might have gone on forever if I didn't send him home or say I had to check on something, because — just like his concerts — he could go on and on forever.

My first husband [Jim Cashmore] was ... I guess I could say he was controlling, but he pretty much instructed me about what to do and where to go, and so forth and so on. I was taking these guitar lessons in the brownstone — we'll say the parlor floor, which is up a level. My husband at that time had his poker group in the basement. We weren't divorced at that point. So there would be the noise of the sort of rise and fall from downstairs, and I suppose also there must have been the sound of music from upstairs.

(James) was seriously alcoholic but that was not defined in those days. There was no such term. It wasn't considered an illness, so I certainly didn't understand it. He died when he was, I think, 43 or 44 years old of cirrhosis of the liver. It was pretty heavy duty. That really affected his personality and so forth, although I didn't understand any of that at the time.

("I Wanna Learn a Love Song") says something like "concrete castle king." I don't know — it makes it sound you're a contractor — but he was a lawyer and also went into the business that had been put in receivership while his father was borough president of Brooklyn. Then, after his father died and he came back to New York, he worked in a corporation counsel's office. He was in Albany for a while, and then he worked in this furniture business.

Right from the beginning, Harry would play songs afterwards and, of course, I guess he was flirting too. Some of his early songs were titles like "Let Me Down Easy," "Stars Shining in Her Hair," I think. "You Weren't in My Plans," I remember that one. He would say, 'If I don't look at you while I'm singing, the song doesn't mean anything.' So that obviously is a set-up.

These [lessons] were off and on because there were times when Harry would call and say he was busy; he had plans. There were times when he didn't show up and so it was theoretically once a week, but it was really off and on. I think it started around the end of January into May. I had decided during this time that I was going to leave. A house had been rented — a ... rental in Point Lookout for the family for the summer — with the idea that my husband at the time would work in the city during the week and come out on weekends. In those days people didn't get divorces and it wasn't really something that you wanted to talk about with your neighbors or your friends.

I told Harry that I would be away for the summer and would let him know when I came back in the fall to pick up the lessons. That was that. I did move out and then I started to proceed towards separation and divorce. I suggested that my husband at the time didn't need to come out on weekends. But anyway we started seeing a counselor, and so forth and so on.

What happened was that Harry called me in this rental on Point Lookout and got the number from the housekeeper, who was still going regularly to the brownstone in Brooklyn Heights. I remember I said I wouldn't be back until the fall and he said he forgot. Through the years if I ever suggested that he tried to find me, he denied it. He said he just thought that he was supposed to keep up the lessons. So it was a mystery exactly why he pursued getting the telephone number and calling.

While I was still in Brooklyn he would stop at the house. This is aside from the guitar lessons. Now the children were home or in nursery school. The housekeeper was there. He would stop by, supposedly on his way to work, at odd times. I mean it could be 11 o'clock in the morning; it could be 1:30 in the afternoon. This is when he had started work on *Legendary Champions*. I thought it was odd. I knew most people went to work from 9 to 5. He'd say he's stopping by on his way to work and he would show me poems. I was kind of a closet poet because that was another thing my husband didn't approve of.

Basically through the summer, there were, I think, occasional phone calls, but the first time that I guess you would say we had a date — only we didn't know it was a date — I had said that I was going to sign up for the poetry series at the YMHA in Manhattan. We were exchanging poetry and that's how when I said I was signing up for the series at the Y, he said, 'Sign me up too ... and I'll pay you later.' So I would say the first date we had was when we both went to a poetry reading at the Y, although it certainly wasn't planned to be a date.

When I left Brooklyn, Jaime was five, Jonathan was three, and Jason was about a year-and-a-half. When I got divorced, I guess it was a couple of years later. They were a couple of years older. I didn't think of myself as dating. In a sense, I was intrigued by his family. I very much romanticized the whole thing. I was living a life at the time that might have been more meaningful if I had had more reason to make it more meaningful. It was very difficult. For example, I would get up on Sunday morning and get the kids ready to go to Sunday school. Then my husband at the time would come down to the door and say, 'What are you doing dressing up those kids and parading them around the neighborhood on Sunday morning? Is this a popularity contest?' You know, he distorted things. It just was getting very, very tricky to have a normal life. Let's say there's a dinner date for Friday evening; he would have me call and say that I was sick, that I had the flu, and we couldn't come. I mean this was a pattern that was building, that you don't know it's a pattern. I didn't really understand a lot of this. I just knew that I was being caged more and more. Criticized more and more.

Not only did (Harry) sing songs after guitar lessons, but

he talked about his family. I became very intrigued. I thought this was real life. I was starting to serve on boards for arts organizations and I had been a teacher and I thought, 'I really want to be an artist.' I just started questioning a lot of things. I just was looking for a more meaningful life. I thought that Harry's family sounded so real, and so interesting, and so intellectually exciting. They were artists, and poets, and writers, and musicians. I was intrigued at being invited into the family.

At the time, Harry was dating other women so I was kind of added to the group, you know. This was not romantic.

I think it was about a year after I met him he actually proposed. He was dating a couple of other people, so it was odd. But then the other thing that happened shortly after that was he got severe asthma for the first time since he was about 11 years old. I always thought that he got asthma because he proposed.

As far as taking on three kids, he didn't blink at that.

**Josh Chapin (Son):** In every way but DNA they were his kids.

**Jason Chapin (Son):** I really remember having two fathers — one, my natural father, who I saw on Christmas and a couple of times throughout the year. He would come out to Point Lookout and sometimes, I think, we would go into the city and go to his apartment. But the person who I considered my real father was Harry because he was around when I was four years old and growing up.

❈ ❈ ❈

## SHOOTING STAR

**Harry Chapin (From a 1980 concert program):** *November, 1968, Sandy Gaston and I are married and set up house in Long Island with her three kids, Jaime, Jono, and Jason. I try a career as a freelance documentary filmmaker and spend my time producing and directing short films for IBM and Time-Life.*

**Fred Kewley (First manager):** He was editing film before he got into music. Back then they had strips of film. It was a physical thing where you'd cut 10 feet of film out and hang it on the wall over here, and then you have six more 10-footers hanging around you. You have to remember what's on each one and then you'd piece it together in the most effective way because it was cut and paste with tape and razor blades. I couldn't get over how complicated that was. You see it when you first cut it out but then you don't see it again until you put it back together. Well that was great training for how he became a great songwriter because he would write a song... and he would edit them a great deal himself.

**Sandy Chapin:** I think while Harry was still at Cornell, he was dating a young woman. It was off and on for a couple of years. It was pretty serious, and her father, I think, was an executive with an airline company. He proposed to Harry that he take a battery of tests, which he arranged someplace in Manhattan. This is a way of measuring what you should do with your life. It's supposed to be very sophisticated. There was a battery of tests and then there was an interview.

The way the story was told to me by Harry — and we

have to recognize that Harry is a storyteller — he says in the interview the guy said, 'We've only had one other person who ranked high in 17 out of 19 facets of this test and he ended up being a dishwasher.' They said there's a problem when you have too many talents competing with each other. So he recommended to Harry he go into film because it would use music and writing and visualization.

**Harry Chapin (From a 1980 concert program):** *A film job surfaces and it's six months in L.A. making airline commercials. Then back to N.Y. to work on boxing films with Cayton, Inc. For the next two-and-a half years I immerse myself in the history of the fight game and by the spring of '67, I tackle a major project,* Legendary Champions, *a theatrical documentary feature. It later wins the New York and Atlanta film festival gold prizes as Best Documentary and is nominated for an Academy Award as Best Feature Documentary.*

**Sandy Chapin:** I think he had one job on Wall Street at one point, but he went to work for his uncle Ricky Leacock, and he did a bunch of short films. He worked on a couple of documentaries and he worked on some short films on boxing called *Boxing Shorts*. Then he ended up working for [Cinematographer] Jim Lipscomb. The job in California was making commercials.

When he came back, of course he didn't have a job. Then he got a job with Jim Jacobs. Jim Jacobs, at that point, had the largest collection of boxing footage in the world and asked Harry to make *Legendary Champions*, which was going to be, I think, *Legendary Champions I* because it went up to a particular date and stopped. Then a second film was going to go on from there that Harry was going to do as well. But then that's when [his] music took off.

**Godfrey Pflager (Editor, *Legendary Champions*):** *Legendary Champions* was totally (Harry's) film. The film did get a nomination for the Best Feature Documentary Oscar. It had a limited run in New York City and Los Angeles.

Harry was a real goer. Many irons in the fire.

**Sandy Chapin:** He got the Academy Award nomination for *Legendary Champions*, so he was working on and off on documentaries. When we got married, all of a sudden he was out of work. He had always been able to go from one job to another. He had said he would never, ever have a 9 to 5 job and the interesting thing is he ended up having a 9 to 4 a.m. job because of all of the different work he was doing.

He would work for five months a year doing documentary films and then he would put aside enough money so that the rest of the year he could just write until he ran out of money again. When we were first married, that's the way he operated. The interesting thing was that for the five months, he worked very hard so then when he stopped he didn't really do much. I mean he was busy in his kind of frenetic way. As the money was running out, he would get frantic. He'd work around the clock. He was always setting deadlines for himself in order to be more productive.

**Harry Chapin (From a 1980 concert program):** *Then it's off to Ethiopia with Jim Lipscomb for a documentary on the World Bank's impact on the underdeveloped world. But again I leave the film business, this time to try writing a Broadway musical. During that summer and fall I write the first four versions of a musical (the ninth version opened on Broadway* *in 1975).*

**Sandy Chapin:** He got a job working for Jim Lipscomb ... to do a documentary for the World Bank about aid in Ethopia and he was gone for about seven months. I think actually he proposed after he came back from Ethiopia. He must have planned it ahead of time because he got his grandmother Lily's ruby ring, which his mother might have been keeping.

Part of the issue here was that when I met Harry, he was 23 years old and I was 31 with three children. At a certain point I said that I didn't think this was such a good idea. We were out in Andover in the summer and I said that I felt that I better move on with my life and be more responsible. I was at that time, I think, back in graduate school and I said, 'I have to take care of the family.' So I guess we were breaking up. Then the next day, he presented this song that he wrote called "It's You, Girl." So that was the end of the break-up.

He was impossible. I mean he was impossible. He did not take no for an answer. That was a good deal of his success with everything he did. He just was relentless. He was an incredible pitchman.

❊ ❊ ❊

**Harry Chapin (From a 1980 concert program):** *By late fall 1970, out of work, I start writing songs again, although in a completely different style. My cinéma vérité experiences and the quest for interesting film stories leads me into a narrative form of songwriting. It is fun writing again, and my brothers Tom and Steve, having formed their own group, are willing to* *perform some of my material.*

**Tom Chapin (Brother):** Harry and I used to go and see (shows) together. One night we went to the Village to see Kris Kristofferson. It was the first time he had come to New York. The opening act was Carly Simon. It was right before she hit with "Anticipation." Russ Kunkel was her drummer, who ended up doing Harry's stuff. It's the Bitter End and we played the Bitter End a bunch, so we sort of feel very confident. Out comes Carly (who) does a great set. We go up to go to the bathroom; we see Carly and Kris making out in the back.

Then Kris comes on and he's a great writer. Kris Kristofferson halfway through goes, 'I was in Chicago last night; heard the best damn train song you ever heard. Please welcome Steve Goodman.' Out comes this guy, blows everybody away. Then he goes off and a big hand and Kris says, 'And here's a friend; please welcome John Prine.' Out comes John Prine who does "Sam Stone." Harry looks at me and goes, 'What are they smoking in Chicago?' Of course that week Steve Goodman got a record contract, which was a big deal in the folk world, because of Kris Kristofferson. That night, I really feel like (Harry) sort of figured he could do this.

**Sandy Chapin:** The whole music thing came about because he rented the Village Gate to raise money to make a small independent film. He wanted to raise about $5,000. Then, of course, one thing led to another and he ended up with a record contract.

**Tom Chapin:** It was called The Chapins. It was the band of Steve, myself, Doug Walker [on guitar], and Phil Forbes.

Harry was working in films but he really wanted to be involved with the music with us. So he'd write these things and we'd rehearse them and work them out. But there were some songs where he wrote long things that we just wouldn't do. He started to get the idea that he really wanted to do them himself.

We get to the summer and we're trying to figure out what to do. The Village Gate has *Jacques Brel is Alive and Well and Living in Paris*, a long-running show. But it ends at 9 o'clock. There's this club empty at 9 o'clock with an empty stage. We go and we rent the club for 400 bucks a week. And we're responsible for that. So our girlfriends run the door and it's The Chapins. At this point, we have a banner made up — *Rock Magazine* called us "The best band I've seen this year." So we said: "The Chapins – The Best Band I've Seen This Year."

Our opening act the first night was Harry by himself, and it was lousy. He couldn't hold it and it just didn't work. The first week he does that. The second week he goes off and he, with Fred's help, starts thinking about what to do. He says, 'I need to have a band.' So he calls up John Wallace, who at this point is a trucker.

**Big John Wallace (Bassist):** He had wanted to get back into music again. His brothers had rented the downstairs at the Village Gate after *Jacques Brel* was over every night for pretty cheap. They were the headliners and I think they had just gotten an Epic record contract or something. I guess even though they were doing some of Harry's songs, he wasn't in the band. I guess then Harry said, 'Screw you guys, I'll get my own band.'

He already knew when he called me that that gig was there. He wanted to put a band together; he wanted to open for them; he wanted a cello. So that's pretty much what happened in that first phone call.

Oh, and I would get 10 bucks a week.

**Tom Chapin:** (Harry) puts an ad in the *Village Voice* for a cello player because of the *Sweet Baby James* album of James Taylor.

**Tim Scott (First cellist):** It's a very good story actually. That's probably the best story of all.

I'm from New York. I went to Julliard for a while and I went to Sarah Lawrence College for a while. I was just about to go to City College when my mother, who was an actress, said, 'Tim, look at this. There's an ad at the back page of the *Village Voice*,' which you always read all the crazy ads on the back page of the *Village Voice*. It said "Cellist wanted for singer-songwriter folk-rock group" — something like that — "Opening at prestigious Village club; Six weeks." So I went on the basis of this — though not many people got into a rock group because of their mother — and auditioned for him at his mother's house in Brooklyn Heights. I always remembered this. I think about three or four cellists auditioned for him and I was one of them. I pretty easily got the job.

He also auditioned for guitar and Ron Palmer got the job over the phone. Then John Wallace was an old childhood friend who hadn't played bass in 20 years. He was still driving a truck at first.

**Big John Wallace:** Food Haulers was the company. They

were in Port Elizabeth, New Jersey. Back then that was just Shop-Rite. While I was there, that's when Shop-Rite and Pathmark had that split, so I was a company driver for a little bit. I [had] just bought a used tractor and started going as an owner-operator. Then my engine blew up, and Harry called.

It was kind of a no-brainer. It wasn't like my life was going so great anywhere else. I was married and my son — the oldest — was born in the spring of '71. It was pretty much around the same time. I was living in an apartment in Orange, New Jersey doing this trucking thing. It was just a pretty grimy kind of depressing life at the time.

**Tim Scott:** The reason he wanted a cello is he thought his voice wasn't particularly beautiful or refined — that a cello would help make it a bit more mellow.

For me, it was a whole different world because I didn't know popular music whatsoever. I was a classical cellist and grew up with almost no popular music. In that way, I was an unusual choice. But I was pretty enthusiastic.

The reason he formed the group was he would try to write songs for his brothers and they didn't necessarily want to do them. They were doing more folk material. But every once in a while they would do one. He had a good number of songs. He had "Taxi." He was pretty often writing songs. It wasn't that difficult for him.

**Fred Kewley:** I had a guitar player who would send his tape to me up from Syracuse, New York, seeing if I could do something for him. We all met in my office in Port Chester, New York for the first time — a cellist and the guitar player who had never met the rest of us.

**Big John Wallace:** Our first gig, I think, was June 29, 1971. This is the way I remember it. We got together for the first rehearsal one week before that. So that was probably June 22nd, in Port Chester, New York. It was actually in Fred Kewley's office. I had never met either Tim or Ron. Ron actually got hired kind of over the phone, which is cool.

It was a pretty tense experience, especially for me, because I was a little bit behind the eight ball with the bass and everything. So it's kind of a whirlwind experience in my mind, but we got a lot done there. Fred was involved pretty heavily in some of those early cello parts. Harry too. He had his own ideas because I think the cello was something he always loved ever since he heard "Fire and Rain," even though I think that was an upright bass playing those drones. But he just thought the cello would be a nice female counterpoint to his kind of gravelly voice. It was a concept that he had for quite a while.

We got along fine. I don't even remember where we stayed or anything else about it. I remember sitting there in the loft, meeting them for the first time, and then just boom — a week later we were on stage. I think four of us on stage and three people in the audience.

We were all into it, you know. As I said, it's new. It's kind of almost overwhelming in a sense because nobody was doing that. Tim comes from the classical world. Ron is up in the small town — Manlius, New York — doing little things here and there. I'm driving a truck. So it was like a whole new career. It was exciting from the get-go.

**Ron Palmer (First guitarist):** I was unemployed but I was playing one night a week in a bar in Syracuse, New York. I was going to try to play for a living for the first time in my life. The owner grew up with Fred Kewley, who was managing The Chapins — the early band with Tom, Steve, Dougie Walker, and Phil Forbes. I sent the tape to Fred Kewley and Fred Kewley played my demo tape to Harry over the telephone. I guess Harry just thought my style would enhance his songs. I couldn't believe that he couldn't find a guitar player in New York City, but anyway that's how it all went down.

[Harry] talked my ear off for about half an hour, 45 minutes, and laid out the whole system of the whole thing that he wanted to do. I had to, of course, think it over, talk it over with my wife, and all that sort of thing. She said, 'Yeah, go ahead.' I mean it might be an opportunity and it might not, but at least at that time they were planning on opening up for The Chapins at the Village Gate. It was going to be like an eight-week gig. Harry offered me $20 a week and a place to stay. So I did it.

**Big John Wallace:** Ron, being from out of town, had to be put up so he got extra money. But we weren't jealous.

**Ron Palmer:** A friend of mine drove me down to Port Chester — that's where the first rehearsals were going to be — and dropped me off. There I was, a little country boy down in the big city wondering what I was doing there for a while.

**Fred Kewley:** We spent a week there. I think we put together eight or nine arrangements. The cellist was a great player but he couldn't arrange. He couldn't improvise. He couldn't come up with parts. Background vocals were important, so the part I played in it was actually arranging most of that, all his vocals. I wrote almost every cello part, I think, and the guy learned it.

When Harry's group got up there and performed, they sounded an awful lot like our college singing group. That's kind of an interesting tie, I think, with the arrangements and the vocals doing what they were doing and the cello acting as another voice.

**Ron Palmer:** The cellist that we had, Tim Scott, was classically trained. He was very unfamiliar, we'll say, with pop music. So Harry and Fred both wrote his lines for him. Of course John Wallace came up with his own bass tracks. He was a very tasty bass player. But Harry gave me carte blanche to come up with my own parts. That was very gratifying to me as far as being able to put my creativity into Harry's music. The guitar parts and everything, that was all my own creations and Harry was very generous to have me do it. I don't think it would have been as successful as it was if anybody was telling me what notes to play here or what notes to play there. I was very satisfied with that situation.

**Fred Kewley:** We got down there for the first night and Harry was the opening act. There were three people in the audience and the four of them on the stage. Harry could hardly talk. His voice was shot from all the rehearsals. Kind of a rough start. But it was nice because we'd get on the phones during the day and call everybody. Eventually we got record companies to come down.

"HELLO, HONEY, IT'S ME"

**Tom Chapin:** By three or four weeks later, people were coming to see him. It was that good.

**George Ball (Cast member, *Jacques Brel is Alive and Well and Living in Paris*):** I got to hear a lot of great, great music that I probably wouldn't have paid to hear. One night there are two bands. The featured band was Tom Chapin's band. He had a real heavy electric rock band at the time and opening for him was his brother Harry. I was blown away. I became completely captivated by this music and these songs because, as an actor, I loved these story songs he sang — "Dogtown" and on, and on, and on. They were there for like two weeks and I was down there every single night.

At a given point in there somewhere, I told him how much I loved what he did and we sort of became buddies. He would come to me on his way in and say, 'Listen,

I need some people to yell tonight. I got some big time agents in the house tonight.'

(Harry) was clean shaven. Very sort of countrified—jeans and plaid shirts, that sort of thing. Very loose. As time went on, more people started to show up. I think some word got out and the word was not about his brother's band. It was about him. It was about his stuff.

**Ron Palmer:** I can remember some of (the songs); probably not all of them. "Could You Put Your Light On, Please" was one of them. A song called "And the Baby Never Cries," and I think "Greyhound" we were working on. "Everybody's Lonely" was another song, and "Sometime, Somewhere Wife," and "Any Old Kind of Day," and "Dogtown." I think that might have been about it. Had about seven songs down in that one week.

**Stanley Snadowsky (Co-Owner, The Bottom Line):** When we were opening up the Bottom Line, (Harry) was doing performances at the Village Gate. I walked over there a few times and caught him when he was just starting, and then I followed him. He was just the consummate performer and the songs were wonderful. Very much like Simon & Garfunkel with their five albums.

**From "Harry Chapin Sings Gorgeous Ballads,"** *The New York Times* **– July 24, 1971:** *His songs ping-pong between the lovely and the weird. A simple polished folk with the added body of the cello. His ballads, notably "And the Baby Never Cries" and "Put Your Light On" [sic] are gorgeous. When he steps afield, as in "Dogtown," about a seaport where departing sailors left their women with big dogs for protection, then never returned, he can be a bit awesome.*

*This is smooth folk, certainly, not pop in any way but polished nicely. It is necessary to mention that only because the recent spate of nasal country singers has predisposed much of the folk audience against hearing traditionally "good" voices. Harry Chapin has one, and writes well.*

**Fred Kewley:** We got the *New York Times* critic to agree to come down and the day he was coming down, the FBI had rifles out at Kennedy Airport and they shot some guy. It was a big front-page story. That guy came down there that night and he walked in the place. He was just out of it. He came in there with his girlfriend and he sat down with her and pretty much leaned his head on the table. He was gone for the night. But the girl was awake and she loved what Harry was doing. The next day we had this rave review from this guy that never saw the show — because the girl liked it.

The airport story started on Page One of the *Times* and went into the D section, say D12; that was the second half of that story and right underneath was "Harry Chapin Is Unbelievable." So the review was placed where an awful lot of people saw it because of that big story at the airport. It meant a lot because all of a sudden to have that kind of review really gives you credibility when you're calling these labels and these other people.

We blew it up and mounted it on a board and put it up on the sidewalk. Before the show we'd all be up there trying to get people to come in, buy a ticket, and watch the show. I had a banner made with "The Chapins" on it, and that thing was out there for many weeks. So yeah, we were out there like carneys trying to get the crowd to come in and we got some money.

I got to tell you, that first night with three people in the audience and four of them on the stage; those numbers are accurate. (Harry) gave almost as much as he would have given if it would have been 20,000 people. If he was on the stage and he was making music, he would do it 100 percent. Many nights at the Village Gate, through those weeks, we'd have small crowds. Once in a while we had bigger crowds, but he would do the same thing every night no matter what it was. He just knew one way to do it and that was the best he could and with full energy. He wouldn't get the blues with only three people in front of him.

**Ron Palmer:** After we had our demo tape and started getting some write-ups, that's when Harry and Fred started hitting the record companies and started getting some of them to come there and listen. God, right from the beginning we started getting offers.

Some of them were pretty strange. The guy that owned Vanguard Records, he wanted Harry but he didn't want the rest of the band. Harry cooled that real quick. At the end when we got in the bidding war between Jac Holzman and Clive Davis, that was a pretty exciting week or two, I can tell you. That's how it all got started, and Harry was the mastermind behind all this. He understood the business very clearly and knew what had to be done and where to get a foot in the door.

Harry had a slogan. He said: 'If you want to be a success, you got to be willing to make an ass of yourself.'

**Sandy Chapin:** He called the different record companies and said, 'This is Fred Kewley and I want to talk to you about this sensational new singer,' and so forth and so on. He did this big pitch and, of course, it was Harry doing it. He called a number of people, and he would always befriend the secretaries in the front office and then he would get to talk to the various record people. But in one case somebody recognized his voice ... and said, 'Ha, this is Harry Chapin!'

He was fearless. He was shameless. He was relentless.

**Tim Scott:** Someone came from Elektra Records, Ann Purtill — the first record was dedicated to her. She heard us and liked us very much. Elektra, with Jac Holzman, gave us the best deal and we thought because it was a smaller label that we might get treated better. In fact, it was a very small label. I remember they had Bread and a couple of other groups. We decided to go with them because we would have more personal attention. Columbia we really thought about.

**Rex Fowler (Musician, Aztec Two-Step):** Ann was a dear, dear person. Harry was her first big signing. Ann was a big fan of Harry's and she was a big fan of ours, obviously, because she signed us. She was very passionate about both acts.

**Ron Palmer:** I remember the feeling I think that we all had the night down at the Village Gate when Clive Davis came in with like 30 people that worked for him — lawyers and accountants and all that stuff. They came pouring in; came climbing out of limousines out front and came piling in. I remember thinking, 'Oh my God, this is something else.'

I just had to keep pinching myself to see if I wasn't dreaming. I mean I had no idea something like this was going to happen. It was like living in a fairy tale there for a while.

**Big John Wallace:** I remember Harry being really excited about it — 'Oh Clive said this, and Jac said this, and Clive said this.' He was definitely loving it in the moment and appreciating it, realizing it was special.

**Tom Chapin:** What happened was that Clive had made him an offer and they said yes. Then (Harry) calls up Jac and Jac says, 'You're crazy — no, no, no!' Jac's in California.

Six a.m., there's a knock on Harry's door. He's living with Sandy out on Long Beach, and there's Jac Holzman. He walks in and says, 'I'm not leaving until you sign with me. Here's what I'll give you — I'll produce the record. I won't release a record a month before or a month after your record. I will push this record.'

Harry signs with Jac Holzman.

**Fred Kewley:** The details of the contract that Jac offered really were much more lucrative over time. You probably know this, but we got a clause in there where if we used the Elektra recording studios in California we wouldn't be charged any studio costs whatsoever. Totally unheard of.

Clive couldn't get over that when he learned it.

**Ron Palmer:** Jac gave us $40,000 out front and if we did two albums and didn't like the way Elektra was treating us ... we could walk out of this contract. Otherwise, we were in for the long haul. But that one escape clause was pretty neat, although none of us even thought about that. Plus the fact that we wouldn't have to pay for (studio time) out of royalties. I mean the word was — at the time — that was the best record deal for a brand new act.

**Jackson Browne (Musician):** As a record company president, (Jac) was the shit. He was deeply influential. He signed Paul Butterfield. He signed The Doors. He signed Koerner, Ray & Glover.

(Elektra) wasn't just a pop record company. In fact, it wasn't a pop record company at all until he got The Doors.

**Niles Siegel (Former album promotion man, Elektra Records):** When a radio station got the envelope in the mail with the Elektra Records logo on the label; that's the one that got opened first.

**Sandy Chapin:** It turned out later that Jac Holzman knew that that was his swan song. That was the last artist he was ever going to sign. And because he won the battle with Clive Davis, he had to show that he was right. That's why he produced the [first] album and promoted it to the extent that he did. So that was a nice combination of breaks for Harry.

**Fred Kewley:** I'll tell you what the big difference was, and this was why we were in the business at the time. It was all about the music. Jac Holzman loved the music. Clive Davis, if he talked about the music, he talked about it very little. But Jac loved it. He had it in his car. He had all of Harry's demos memorized. He was the kind of guy who would put out "Taxi" as the first single where Clive Davis never would put out a six-and-a-half minute song as a single.

He was a really good man — one of the really good people

in the record business. Jac never upped the deal; he only matched it in terms of the front money. But he got real creative with all his other clauses.

Jac put his whole reputation behind Harry.... He put me in business. He put Harry in business.

# CHAPTER 3

## *HEADS & TALES*

**From a 1972 Elektra Records advertisement for *Heads & Tales*:** *Harry is ... a music and a band. Harry is a storyteller and — if I may coin a word — an évocateur. His songs, in which "Taxi" is a superb example, are a marvelous unity of memorable melody and finely wrought lyrics.... He is a major discovery and we expect him to have the same kind of initial public impact as did Carly Simon.*

**Fred Kewley (First manager):** Jac put himself down as the producer of the first album. He was in the studio with us for a couple of months doing that album.

**Big John Wallace (Bassist):** (Recording) took a long time. I think we were there for a couple of months for that first album.

You're under the microscope. I was very self-critical at the time, so I didn't like anything I was doing. It's almost like you're playing defensively or you're not trying to lose rather than being on top of it and having fun playing, you know. That's just the way it was for me, I'm not talking about anybody else. Especially because we had the great Russ Kunkel [on drums]. That was the part of it that was really cool for me; to play with somebody as good as he was. It's like having kind of big, strong arms holding everything together.

**Tim Scott (First cellist):** We had the luxury of spending a lot of time [in the studio]. (Harry) would go over things quite a bit until he got the voice just the way he wanted it. I remember one song called "Same Sad Singer," which Jac Holzman was actually the engineer for, because we did it like very late in the middle of the night. We did three tracks of the cello. It was very tiring. He was somewhat driven in the studio and somewhat of a perfectionist. I don't remember like hating him, I know that. I don't remember that being a big problem, but we took our time. We never rushed in the studio. I remember we had this drummer, Russ Kunkel, who was some well-known L.A. drummer there and was very good. That certainly helped us out some.

**Bob Heimall (Former art director, Elektra Records):** Harry was different than any other artist I worked with in that he really didn't come across as a recording artist. He came more across as a regular guy, businessman, 9 to 5, go to work kind of guy. He'd come into my office and he'd say, 'Do you have a desk? I got a song idea; could I use one of your typewriters?' My secretary would get up. He'd sit at the desk for a half hour and just talk and write songs and do business.

Jac said, 'Bob, we got to treat this artist different. This is not your normal singer-songwriter-type artist. His stories are songs. They are like books. You open a book and you read it.' That's what I tried to do when I did his album cover. You look at the "Taxi" album cover, it really tells a story. I mean it's got a die cut in the front so as you open the package, it reveals more about Harry and different parts of his art and his music.

**Niles Siegel (Former album promotion man, Elektra Records):** One day, Jac comes into my office. He stands over my desk and he says, 'Niles, I spent a lot of money on this record. I couldn't afford to pay a producer; I had to do it myself. You got to bring this one home. It's got to be a hit.' And I said, 'OK, if that's the way you want to be about it, then let's go for it.'

I loved it, and I loved Harry. Harry was a wonderful guy.

❈ ❈ ❈

**Harry Chapin (From a 1980 concert program):** *The end of '70 arrives, there are no film jobs and the movie industry is an economic disaster area. My daughter Jenny is six months on the way to being born and I panic. I set into New York City to sign up for a hack license. On the way, I meet an old girlfriend who has married money instead of becoming an actress, and I contemplate the irony of "flying in my taxi." But the day I'm supposed to start driving fate again intervenes and I'm offered three film jobs. Relieved, I plunge back into work, but find that the songs are still coming.*

**Sandy Chapin (Wife):** He'd pick up $100 here, $100 there for something, but the money ran out. All of a sudden there was a recession. There was nobody looking for him for a documentary and that's when he got a hack license. And the day that he got assigned to this garage, three different film jobs came in and then he did some training films for IBM.

He never drove a cab.

**Ron Palmer (First guitarist):** It was Harry who wrote the song ["Taxi"] and was still writing it when we went in the studio. It was from something he experienced himself because he did want to be a pilot. I'm sure he's probably had a few girlfriends and got hurt just like anybody else does. He used his imagination to put it together into a song.

**Robert Mrazek (Friend; Former U.S. representative):** His songs usually involved loss and the loss of one's hopes when they are young. They get older and things don't turn out the way they planned, which is the foundation of "Taxi." "She was going to be an actress, and I was going to learn to fly," and neither one of them are happy in their lives. There's this poignant moment at the end where she gives him a $20 bill and he no longer has the pride to reject it and simply stuffs it in his pocket and goes on. A loss —unlike Harry's life. One of failure.

He gave you these peoples' lives—broken as they were.

**Fred Kewley:** "Taxi" was two songs that he edited together. That whole John Wallace thing in the center was another song he had been working on.

**Niles Siegel:** The entire industry revolved around singles at that point.

Harry's record was a particularly difficult one because it was like forever. It went on for a couple of months. It just never ended.

We had real problems with ("Taxi") because as much as people loved it, one of the major markets in this country, in terms of Top 40, was San Francisco, and he was driving his cab in "Frisco." "Frisco" was derogatory. We had to fight like hell and beg and plead and practically get on our knees to get that record played in San Francisco so we could make [the] Top 10. San Francisco wouldn't touch it.

I remember this so well because it was such a battle and it was so difficult. The reality of it was the program director at the Top 40 station in San Francisco was a guy named Sebastian Stone, who happened to be one of my dearest friends. [He] said, 'Niles, I can't play this record. They're going to chew me up and spit me out here if I play this record — calling San Francisco "Frisco." I can't do it.' Eventually the record was selling so well and it was just taking off so beautifully that he had to. But that was one of the problems, the length. Nobody wanted to play anything longer than three minutes because it didn't fit the format.

**Bob Zachary (Former producer, Elektra Records):** Yeah, I'm sure it was hard. But Elektra was pretty famous for getting kind of oddball things. I mean one of our biggest hits was Judy Collins singing "Amazing Grace." At that time, who would have ever thought that a hymn would become a Number One record? Harry told stories and storytellers make the best songwriters. I produced a guy named Paul Siebel and he was another great one. He told stories. A lot of Elektra guys are like that. Even Jim Morrison — he was a poet.

**Eric Bazilian (Musician, The Hooters):** I remember when "Taxi" came out, how the characters were so alive to me. (Harry) was actually one of the very few "troubadours" of the time of whom I never tired of.

**Fred Kewley:** I remember the summary of the conversation was, 'Give me three for the radio and the rest of the album you can have.'

I can say that early on he was writing songs that people liked that were not necessarily at all designed for the radio. The first hit he had was "Taxi," which broke all the rules. Of course "American Pie" did really well too, but it was really exceptional to have a six minute and 44 second single on the radio because the big stations then — and there were eight of them that really mattered in the country — if it was over three-and-a-half minutes they just said they wouldn't play it. So that was something we learned.

**Niles Siegel:** It didn't sound like anything else. It wasn't pop; it wasn't folk; it wasn't country; it wasn't rock. It was stories, and stories about real life. You know, "she was going to be an (actress)," and here he is driving a taxi. I mean these are real stories. These are stories about people who didn't make their dreams. So they were really difficult and by the time you pounded it into the program director's head and the music director's head what was really going on here, they finally got it. They finally got that Harry was telling real-life stories.

Very few people told real-life stories like that.

**Ron Palmer:** It's a great song and it got us a foot in the door because it did get up on the charts.

**Fred Kewley:** I'll say that first album did well. We got ourselves in business.

**Sandy Chapin:** I actually wrote a poem about it. It was

like (Harry) was going to move to Mars. We had such a close relationship over writing and words. He worked on everything I wrote and I worked on everything he wrote. I mean it was so close and so invigorating.

I remember when we first went to Jac Holzman's place in upstate New York and Jac brought him into his home studio. I saw that machine with all those boards and buttons and I thought, 'Oh, uh-oh.' It was really, really scary.

**Jono Chapin (Son):** I remember little things. There was this big record contract, and the next thing you know we got a hand-me-down pool table from the Elektra record company. There was a point where I remember seeing some gold record framing — you know, frames that went upon the wall.

**Tom Chapin (Brother):** The whole thing was not only surprising; it was thrilling. The thing that's interesting about this is it's not like this is an unknown. I never felt like, 'Why isn't this me?' That didn't even occur to me. I mean I was already doing *Make a Wish*. Harry bought his house because I got him the job as the writer on *Make a Wish* that same summer actually. It was a very fertile time. I'm filming all day, five days a week in New York City — the same time we're doing the Village Gate at night.

He wrote "Circle" for that and a bunch of songs. So it was surprising and wonderful and thrilling. It was like, 'Wow, look at this happen,' but it wasn't like, 'That should be me.' That didn't even occur to me or Steve. We grew up with Harry. Nothing was surprising with Harry. My quote that the family loved at the time was, 'Two's company, Harry's a crowd,' and we used it all the time. I mean in some ways we were incredibly competitive, but I mean the music is what we did together. It was a collaborative event.

**Ron Palmer:** We went out there in the first part of December and we worked right up until a Christmas break or something. Then later on we had to go back to Los Angeles and finish a couple of things or change a couple of things. Then it was like a month or two later when we went out on our first tour.

**Big John Wallace:** I remember specifically when I touched (*Heads & Tales*) for the first time. We were in San Francisco. A carton of them came in and I opened it up and held it in my hand for the first time — the shrink-wrapped version. That was an amazing feeling. I'll never forget that. That's when you really got a sense of the accomplishment of what just happened.

Put it this way, financially the first year we made $6,000 or something but, of course, that was just half a year. Year two, we made $11,000 or something and it kept inching up like that. We played gigs here and there. I guess we started to do colleges, but this is before the record came out. The first gig we played after the record came out, I remember, was in Champaign-Urbana. The audiences had responded tremendously to Harry all along. It's because he lays it all out there, you know. You can tell he's giving it everything he can, so the responses are always good. But we walked out on stage this night after the record had been released and the crowd just went nuts. Like a standing ovation when we were walking out. We just kind of looked at each other and said, 'Wooo, things are a little different now!'

**Jackson Browne (Musician):** I saw (Harry) at the record company. Of course he was unmistakably him. He was great. He seemed exactly like the guy in the songs. He seemed very friendly and down-to-earth. And kind.

**Tim Scott:** We did a tour for Elektra Records. We opened for Carly Simon at the Troubadour. What I remember about that is she introduced her friend James Taylor, who was very big at the time. We opened for Cheech & Chong at the Bitter End in New York. We opened for the comedian David Steinberg, I think, at a big comedy club in Chicago and then around the country quite a bit. Then we just toured around a lot of college campuses or odd places around the country. College campuses, gyms, that type of thing. Some very nice concert halls too, as I recall — Kleinhans Music Hall in Buffalo; a big one in St. Louis.

As far as I can recall, we never did one cover song. Never. A hundred percent original material.

**John Oates (Musician, Hall & Oates):** We did actually play together. When Daryl and I first started, and I believe it was in '72, we opened for Harry Chapin at the Troubadour in L.A.

He was a really cool guy. We actually got him to come on stage with us and do this really funny, kind of crazy song that Daryl and I had written. It was called "Whistling Dave." We never recorded it. It was almost like a jug band song and I guess he had heard us doing it during soundcheck as a joke because we weren't really playing it in our set. For some reason, I think he liked it and he said something about it. We said, 'Hey, do you want to come up and sing it? We'll do it.' We were opening for him but he came up during our encore, which is very rare for a headliner to do that. I thought that was really cool.

**Fred Kewley:** We got that album done and Jac started going to the trades — the *Billboards* and the rest of it — talking about Harry over and over, doing all kinds of interviews. Just like the biggest hype you ever saw — that Harry Chapin is the next big thing.

Then Elektra had a convention and it was in Phoenix. Harry was going to perform for the first time there where the industry would see him, including all the artists on Elektra Records, and all their managers, and all the agents, and all the rest of it. It was kind of a big inside deal at this Elektra convention and Jac had actually laid everything on the line. I can tell you that every time there was a situation like that where it was a pressure situation where Harry had to do really well to not make it a total fiasco, he always came through every time. He just knocked them over there at that convention.

**Rex Fowler (Musician, Aztec Two-Step):** Harry was, as you can imagine, a larger than life character. He was Kennedy-esque.

"Taxi" had really made some noise. The shows were all sold out. I don't know if that many people were aware of us. We did certainly bring some fans into that, but our record had just come out. We were promoting the record whereas Harry had already made his splash. He was headlining, bringing people in. If we had headlined, we would have had 15, 20 people. It was always sold out.

It was very exciting because the place was packed every time you went out on stage. We always held our own.

His fan base was very respectful and enthusiastic about us, so that was nice. We had a smattering of fans in there because we were just getting some airplay on FM radio as well. It was a nice double bill.

**Fred Kewley:** After "Taxi" came out, we went out to do the first *Johnny Carson* show. He's backstage behind the curtains and the air conditioning is up full blast. Everybody is shaking in their boots — nerves, cold — and the curtain opens and there you are. Whatever he did, he did that equally well to the convention. The crowd went crazy.

We were out in the parking lot after the show packing up and Fred de Cordova, the producer of the show, came out. He said, 'Guys, we have absolutely never done this before, but what are you doing tomorrow night? Can you come back tomorrow night and do it again?' I think (Harry) was definitely the first at that point, and probably the only artist like that, to do two *Tonight Shows* in a row, especially being his first and second.

**Ron Palmer:** Johnny Carson did a little fibbing with this deal. What happened was we were scheduled to do it that one night and they had a cancellation the next day. They knew we were in town, so they called us and asked us if we'd like to come back. Of course, Johnny Carson blew it all up like we were back by popular demand — that sort of thing — which was good for us, for sure. But the truth of the matter was they had a late cancellation the next day.

**Sandy Chapin:** I always had this romantic picture of Harry; of the American troubadour that traveled around the country carrying his songs. He stood up and played his songs. He went to the college or downtown where he hung out, and he picked up another story, and wrote another song and took it to the next town, and so on and so forth. I mean his songs cover real people and real places all over the United States.

**Bob Heimall:** I was going out to California to shoot an album cover for the group Bread's *Manna* [album], and Harry was going out there to record — do some other business with his band or they had some sessions. We just shared the jet and it was another funny experience. Harry was talking to the pilot. He says, 'I know this great restaurant that makes these great pastrami' — or some kind of — 'sandwiches in St. Louis.' So I don't know how they arranged it, but they called ahead through the tower somehow and got the sandwiches delivered to the airport. We landed somewhere in the middle of the United States and picked up lunch from a deli that Harry recommended and we all ate lunch on the way out to L.A. It was just a neat experience. It was fun. I talk about it because it was very unique and it doesn't happen that often. Whatever he said he would follow through on. He was a very self-confident guy.

**Fred Kewley:** I got a call from our agent early in the game. We were all up in New York. He said, 'I have an offer for you to open up for The Temptations in El Paso, Texas tomorrow night.' I called Harry and he says, 'Yeah, let's do it.' So we just rounded everybody up on like 24 hours notice — if that — flew down to El Paso, did the show, and flew back. The agent said, 'You're the only act that I got or ever heard of that would have done that.' That started with Harry. I mean he was the one who would do that.

**Tim Scott:** What he did with us ... that I did appreciate

[was] the financial arrangement. From all the concerts, we split the money four ways and he just got the money from royalties if other people sang his songs, which does seem completely fair. We were treated very well in that way.

**Big John Wallace:** This is one of the first things that he did. I guess maybe we were in a diner in Brooklyn Heights. He kind of laid it all out. He said, 'Guys, I don't have any money.' He said, 'I can't pay you money now. We're not going to be able to have any money until we start making it ourselves, so I can't give you anything now. But what I'll give you is a straight four-way split. Everybody gets 25 [percent], including me.' And that was it. That was a handshake deal — boom. That was it, and that's the way it stayed. Of course management and agents got their cut off the top, but he never reneged or tried to renege on that deal.

But he also said — loyalty was very important to him — 'If I fire you for any reason, you'll keep getting whatever you've earned. But if you leave, you're going to forfeit it.' So at the end of three-and-a-half years when the Broadway show came up and Ron left, he left knowing that he wasn't going to see any more money.

**From a 1972 *Rolling Stone* review of *Heads & Tales*:** *Harry's story songs are his worst.... "Taxi" is, of course, the most famous song on* Heads & Tales, *and that's unfortunate because it's the album's second or third worst song, and a veritable textbook of lyrical, melodic, and production errors. The opening melody is merely banal, but more seriously, Harry doesn't know how to construct a story (Interestingly, Harry's publishing company is called Story Songs, and the word "tales" a part of the LP title). His method is to build up an ac-*

cretion of superfluous and irrelevant detail which effectively halts any narrative momentum.... Certainly you shouldn't be prejudiced against Harry on the basis of the unavoidable "Taxi." Harry's comprehensive resume also includes some time spent as a stock broker. Maybe his next album will tell us a story about "that."

❊ ❊ ❊

## SNIPER AND OTHER LOVE SONGS

**Fred Kewley:** Now we're hotshots because we knew what we were doing. I produced the [second] album and it was *Sniper [and Other Love Songs]*. We made an album for us that had a lot of great stuff. I think that song "Sniper" — if you get a chance, you put that on a good sound system, just turn the lights down, and get between the speakers and you'll see it's an amazing experience. But it wasn't a three-minute single. We mixed that for 24-hours straight and there were four of us all assigned various jobs mixing it.

**Josh Chapin (Son):** I know I'm in trouble if I listen to "Sniper" and it doesn't knock me out or hit me on some level like inside.

**Big John Wallace:** I think Steve [Chapin] feels the same way that, in many ways, it's Harry's masterpiece.

**Marie "Peachie" Marsden (Friend):** "A Better Place to Be" is about an old guy and a young girl and they just find each other. They are both lonely so why shouldn't they be together? What's wrong with that?

**Gordon Lightfoot (Musician):** I remember one time I was playing in Britain. I was staying at a hotel there for about three or four days in London. I played (Harry's) first couple of albums. I played them over and over again and I learned that song "A Better Place to Be." That was one of my all-time favorites by him. It's the story in the song that grabs you and then, of course, the melody and the chords and everything that goes with that.

**Paul Layton (Musician, The New Seekers):** At this time, our record producer David Mackay was looking for songs for our next album. Either ("Circle") was submitted to him by the publisher or David was aware of the song from Harry Chapin's recording. It was recorded in 1972 at Morgan Studios in North West London where Cat Stevens recorded. I remember it well because for the extended version ... we went out onto the street and rounded up members of the public to come in and do some singalong choruses and hand claps for the end fade out.

It was most successful in the U.K. where it reached Number Four in the charts and remained in that position for four weeks; and a total of 16 weeks in the charts. It was in the top 50 bestselling singles of 1972.

("Circles") is a highlight of our concerts and I have it on good authority that it remains the fans' favorite. In the U.K. ... I guess the message is timeless as it has such a poignant lyric. Life does seem to keep going round and round in circles.

**Ron Palmer:** Harry wanted (*Sniper and Other Love Songs*) to be a double album. Fred Kewley and Harry basically produced that album, and then, of course, we had produced enough for a double album. But Jac Holzman just up and said, 'Harry, the world is not ready for a double Harry Chapin album.' So that went down the wayside.

**From a 1972 *Rolling Stone* review of *Sniper and Other Love Songs*:** *The most that I can say for this kind of wretched excess is that it is impossible for one to remain emotionally neutral to it. Chapin has the courage of his convictions, and the sheer insistency with which he advertises his case of emotional diarrhea does carry some energy and invoke some sympathy.... No doubt some will find all of this socially meaningful and even personally cathartic. Harry goes to great lengths in trying to evoke a dark, inchoate strain of American life and make it "art." What does him in is his own overweening self-pity, which distorts and demeans his apparently sincere intentions.*

**Jason Chapin (Son):** My father took a lot of criticism from music critics. They didn't think he was that good and they weren't impressed with his recordings and his concerts.

He wouldn't say anything to us like, 'This person's horrible because he wrote a negative review.' In his concerts he would make fun of himself and say, 'This is a song that I hope you enjoy more than the critics.' He was always trying to win them over. He would do lots of interviews with either print or radio or television. He was always trying to get them to appreciate him and recognize his talents. But he also was aware that a lot of them didn't think that he was as good as his fans did.

**Dave Marsh (Friend; Music critic):** I never liked Harry's music much. At the same time, he was a very, very important friend to me. He really came from a different place than I did. I'm coming from R&B slash rock and roll; he's coming from folk and theater music. I think his stuff was very dramatic and was inclined not to be very subtle musically. He was perfectly happy to hit you over the head with a concept.

**Gordon Lightfoot:** We respected our talent. We knew that we had guts. We knew that we had the drive. Of course you're never quite sure about your writing ability until something happens, but I think there was a really good mutual respect there in our writing ability.

I certainly respected (Harry's) — I'll tell you that.

**Gerry Beckley (Musician, America):** The [1972 Grammy Award for Best New Artist] category was Loggins and Messina, The Eagles, ourselves, Harry, and John Prine, so that's a pretty deep bench for "Best New Artist."

There was a lot of lovely, incredibly unique stuff happening in the late-'60s and early-'70s. One of the great genres is the storyteller song. ("Taxi") was a fascinating record.

When I speak about being at Warner Brothers in those years, I always mention three artists — Ry Cooder, Randy Newman, and Van Dyke Parks. There's three very shining examples of artists somewhat like Harry that were very unique.

There was a place for artists at that time. Labels were proud to have people like Van Dyke even if his numbers weren't enough to chart the records. These guys were of immense talents and went on to prove themselves in many other capacities. I think Harry clearly was in that category of very, very unique talent.

## A BETTER PLACE TO BE

**Sandy Chapin:** I ended up seeing a house advertised in the *New York Times*.... We looked at the house and it was a wonderful, wonderful ramshackle place to raise a family. It was a complete wreck. We got an engineer's report; the highest mark it had was a D. We did sell the house in Point Lookout and then Jac Holzman gave this advance. That's how we got the house because we didn't have any money back then.

The thing was we were risk takers. We were totally unafraid because if you've been poor and it was OK, you can go there again. We said, 'Well if we can't keep up the house; if we can't manage; if it's too much, then we'll just go back where we were and that will be OK.' So it was kind of crazy but it wasn't scary. It was just before school started in 1972. *Heads & Tales* was out.

We moved to a huge eight bedroom, 12-room old Victorian house. There was a screen porch off the kitchen. There was a bed and a dresser for each of us, including Harry and me. That was it — that was the entire house. Nothing in the living room. Nothing in the dining room.

I had finally found this house and I decided it would be a great place to raise a family and Harry had said, 'I'm sure I'll like anything you do.' I said, 'Well we have to put down a deposit, so you have to see the house now.' So we took this trip from Point Lookout with the kids and we drove down Locust Lane [in Huntington Bay, Long

Island]. Every house was pristine and had professional landscaping and those kind of square cornered bushes in front of the houses.

As we're driving down Harry says, 'I told you I would like anything you picked out, but I don't have a good feeling about this.'

We're walking around the house with this real estate lady and we go into the kitchen and there's an 1890 iron stove in the kitchen. (Harry) walks into the kitchen and he turns to the lady and he said, 'We'll take the house,' which you don't do. I mean Harry was pretty young then; you don't do that. You find fault with the house; find all the problems; you list the problems; you offer half as much as they're asking. He just turns to her and says, 'We'll take the house.' That was our introduction to Huntington.

It had no number when we moved there but then they got sophisticated later and divided some of the lots on the street. It ended up being number 36. Thirty-six Locust Lane.

**Jono Chapin:** It was big but my mom filled it with a lot of secondhand antique-type furniture. It was pretty eclectic.

**Josh Chapin:** What I loved about it is it was definitely big. I mean you could call it a mansion, I guess, but it was to be used. I really loved growing up in a house like that. There was nothing ostentatious about it. I had a larger house than most of my friends, but when everybody was home there was no sense of extra rooms or high ceilings or anything. It was a very warm place. It was just really wonderful to be in and we always filled it up. There was always house guests and people coming. It just kind of had that energy to it. It was like, 'Hey, you're here; you're at the Chapin house, so enjoy yourself!'

❊ ❊ ❊

## *SHORT STORIES*

**Harry Chapin (From a 1975 concert):** *I have trouble getting my songs on the radio because they're too long, but this is a song that snuck on the charts for about 15 minutes.*

**Fred Kewley:** (*Sniper and Other Love Songs*) was a good album but there was nothing there for radio. That really slowed us down as far as our moving along with (Harry's) career. We knew we had to come up with something to get back on the radio.

Harry wrote "W·O·L·D."

**Sandy Chapin:** After (*Heads & Tales*) was out, as he was touring and doing small clubs all over the country, he made a point of going into radio stations and schmoozing program directors and disc jockeys, which is what led to "W·O·L·D."

**Fred Kewley:** I'm sure we talked about it at the time — 'Write a song of these disc jockeys.' See we were traveling around and having lunches and meetings and interviews with disc jockeys all the time. The noticeable thing about most of those was those conversations were almost entirely about the disc jockeys and almost nothing about Harry Chapin. You know, a lot of egos out there. I think he figured it out that if he wrote a song about disc jockeys, they'd play it. That was a fairly calculated way of getting back on the radio after the second album.

**Robert Mrazek:** "W·O·L·D" is a song about failure. It's about a man who pursues his career as the "morning voice" and loses his family and ends up going farther and farther down the food chain until the end when his professional life is over and there's nothing left in his life. There's a sense of tragedy about that.

**Melanie Marsden (Friend):** My father, he had friends at the phone company. He had all the operators call and request ("W·O·L·D") so that it would flood the station with requests. They wanted it to go gold in Boston.

**Fred Kewley:** "Mr. Tanner," I think, is maybe my favorite song of his and should be a hit but never has been. I say it should be because it's good. I mean his lyrics were always very good, but the lyrics in that thing are just outstanding. He just paints this picture — a very complete picture — in very few words.

**From "Tubridy, a Bass-Baritone, Performs in 2d Recital Here,"** *The New York Times* **– February 17, 1972:** *Martin Tubridy, a bass-baritone who came to Town Hall on Tuesday night to give his second New York recital, performed songs by Beethoven, Schubert, Vaughan, Williams, Britten, and others. He was accompanied on the piano by Mitchell Williams.*

*Mr. Tubridy's voice seemed quite limited in amplitude, range, and flexibility, and it was probably because of this that his interpretations lacked force and strong communicative power.*

*He was well-prepared and sang conscientiously, but the results were not up to generally accepted levels of professional accomplishment.*

**Big John Wallace:** I think it was Harry's idea from the beginning. He read a review about a singer from Dayton, Ohio — Martin Tubridy — and here again, you know, empathizing with the downtrodden little guy who got his ass kicked in the reviews. That's how that one was started.

**Martin Tubridy (Inspiration for "Mr. Tanner"):** I was not aware for many, many years after that Harry Chapin had seen a review I had received from a Town Hall recital I did in the early 1970s and actually had used it as his inspiration for "Mr. Tanner." In the ensuing years after, I found it very hard to believe that there could possibly be a tie-in to my concert which was so many years ago.

In 2016, Howard Fields of the Chapin band contacted me to sing "Mr. Tanner" with the band in Connecticut and confirmed the connection. He also gave the perspective that the song held a special meaning to Chapin fans and to Harry Chapin himself as he had previously received less than favorable reviews regarding his own music from the critics who may have preferred he move closer to rock music. (Harry) had an incredible ability to relate meaningful and moving messages in his thought-provoking songs, such as "Cat's in the Cradle," "Taxi," and "Mr. Tanner."

"Mr. Tanner" is an absolutely beautiful piece that really musically creates a compelling story between listener and storyteller with its own deep feeling of hope as the song is completed. It is a song that honors the gifts we are given and [tells us] to not give up. It has become an honor for me to learn so much more about Harry Chapin and all the profound good that he has done for others that are in need.

**Big John Wallace:** Why ("Fall on your knees" is) in there, I don't remember. That was one of the things that we did in the choir — "O Holy Night."

**Tommie Lee Jackson (Backing vocalist, *Short Stories*):** That was kind of a joke between them in the studio — that he was singing that. Yet he was just so beautiful on "Mr. Tanner."

**Marie "Peachie" Marsden:** (Harry) was still working on

("Mr. Tanner"). We were up in New York at Elspeth's house. His brothers were there and all the brilliant and talented musical people. They said, 'No, it's too Christmasy, the "Fall on your knees." You should take that out.' He's sitting there and he's looking around the room — 'What do you think?' 'Yeah, take it out.' 'And what do you think?'

He turns to [my husband] Zeke and he says, 'What do you think?' Zeke goes, 'I think it's the best part of the song. I love it.' Harry says, 'See that, that's a fan.' He says, 'It's staying in,' because Zeke, I think, represented all the people out there that couldn't get in touch with him and talk to him.

**Tommie Lee Jackson:** I met the guys in REO Speedwagon and their producer, Paul Leka, asked me to come to Connecticut to sing on their [second] album (*R.E.O./T.W.O.*). Of course I jumped at the chance. Later on he called me and said, 'Boy, I'd really like you to sing with this guy, Harry Chapin.'

I really didn't know Harry's music. But I got there and it was so interesting the way he worked. His instructions were, 'Let loose.' He was impressed I could just sing out instead of just sing the notes. He was very encouraging with that. He also had specific ideas about things and I liked that structure because he knew exactly what he wanted on the recording. But he also was open to spontaneity.

I was green. I was still just learning the ropes. But with Harry and the guys, it was kind of like just being one of the guys. Though they treated me like a lady, I was still one of the guys. That made me feel good because I've always been kind of a tomboy in working with musicians. They're all like my big brothers.

I think it took us a week to go through all the things that we played on. I must admit on *Short Stories*, my two favorite songs are "Mr. Tanner" and "Mail Order Annie." I cannot listen to those songs without crying. They just evoked such emotion in me.

**Tom Chapin:** The ones that blow me away are still "Mail Order Annie" — "Mail Order Annie, never mind your crying. Your tears are sweet rain in my empty life." "Old College Avenue," because the melody is just transcendent and it reminds me of us.

Harry used to visit up in Plattsburgh all the time. All the brothers came up there because I was a huge star at the school and it was kind of a favorite place. They'd come up and Harry could date girls, and we could play music. It was really a lovely place to come. My first year up there, I had a double bed and Harry would come in a room that was about the size of a closet and he'd ... sleep on the floor right next to it. So he had: "Old College Avenue. The tiny room and the single bed. The tangled trails of time..." The melody is so transcendent. Very romantic, you know. He has this very romantic side to him that was just really astonishing.

**Big John Wallace:** He would normally bring (songs) in, especially if he felt good about it. I remember a few years later when he brought "Cat's in the Cradle" in and he sang it to us in the dressing room one day before a show. I remember thinking when I heard that, 'Wow, this song sounds great. Something could be here.'

**Tommie Lee Jackson:** It just made me feel like I was really singing and doing what I was meant to do. He would pull that vocal out of you. He was a good coach in the studio. Sometimes producers count more on what you can do and kind of let you loose. He did that but he would also direct and encourage. You could use your imagination, so that was a first for me. It's always nice when you can have somebody that respects that.

It was a short story for me with Harry. But it was lovely.

❊ ❊ ❊

**Big John Wallace:** We all got really close. I mean even one year on the road you're in the trenches. It's kind of like being in the war without getting shot at. You're going through a lot, so you bond. Everybody got along really well, especially even with Harry back then because we were still traveling together. He was part of us. Of course later on, the more and more he had going in his life, then it was a separate thing and we didn't see him as much anymore.

**Tim Scott:** Harry was very fair to us, but I felt he could be very sexist and a little too aggressive in his personality sometimes. I don't want to say conceited exactly, but he just thought he was the greatest songwriter ever and that kind of bothered me.

It was when you left the group that that was it. You didn't get any royalties after that. But that was fine. That was the agreement we had and I always felt that was perfectly fair. Staying with the group another year or two, I might have made a lot of money, you know. But I didn't.

It wasn't acrimonious. I was kind of young at the time and what I recall was I just got tired and decided I wanted to go back and live in one place and all. I wrote them a letter that was accepted perfectly nicely and they got another cellist. I even helped them get the other cellist, so it might have been fairly friendly. I remember forgetting to sign the letter. I was like 22 years old — I didn't know what I was doing. But it was not acrimonious.

**Ron Palmer:** Tim didn't like a lot of things that were going on, so he quit. As far as I know, he's still playing in Portland with the Oregon Symphony Orchestra. That's what he did right after he left here.

**Marie "Peachie" Marsden:** (Harry) had a beard that went under his chin. I used to think, 'It's supposed to be under your chin line,' but that was the style back then — the beard would be under your chin. It looked scraggly. He looked unkempt. But Harry just put clothes on because he had to wear clothes. He ate because he needed energy to keep going.

**Sandy Chapin:** In the beginning when he was on the cross-country tour, he just took off. I mean he was traveling from state to state and moving across countries. Later when my kids were filling out college applications and they had to put down religion, they said 'What am I?' I felt a little badly because even though they had gone to church in Point Lookout, we had never joined a church in Huntington because I said our religion was "Go Find Daddy." I would pack them up at the end of the school week and we'd go to Rochester, or we'd go to Philadelphia. We would go to where Harry was. Sometimes I had a babysitter and I went on the road. It varied according to their vacation time and schedules, and so forth, but I mean mostly it was my job to have a relatively stable home life and keep up the score.

# CHAPTER 4

## CAT'S IN THE CRADLE

**Harry Chapin (From a 1980 concert program):** *Songs, albums, concerts, and benefits followed in '73 and '74. By then my son Josh was born, Sandy wrote the lyrics for "Cat's in the Cradle," and in December 1974 it became the Number One record in the country.*

**Melanie Marsden (Friend):** Everyone thinks Cat Stevens wrote "Cat's in the Cradle."

**Ingrid Croce (Wife of musician Jim Croce):** I've had a few fans write to tell me "Cat's in the Cradle" was one of their favorite Jim Croce songs. I personally like it myself. It reminds me a bit of Cat Stevens too — his "Father and Son" song. It reflects a stage in life when young people want to separate from their folks and become their own person. It's a tough time and they both wrote about it in a very poignant way, from different points of view.

I think Harry's music, Cat Stevens', and Jim's really capture the human condition. They are all great storytellers.

**Stanley Snadowsky (Co-owner, The Bottom Line):** If you listen to the song "Cat's in the Cradle," it's a story of almost any young man trying to better himself. He has to sacrifice something. What you sacrifice is your family. It's unfortunate. You don't mean to do it. And when you establish yourself you find your son is just like (you). It's a splice of life.

**Josh Chapin (Son):** It was a message to (Harry) but (my mom) wrote it as a poem about her first husband's relationship with his father. My dad saw it and it obviously helps him to resonate with the audience if he says it's about him. It's not, but obviously there's something about him singing it that makes it real.

**Sandy Chapin (Wife):** I remember when I showed him "Cat's in the Cradle." He sort of dismissed it.... Then when it came up again after Josh was born, he latched onto it and then sat right down and put music to it. It was kind of interesting that [he] saw it in a whole different light.

Writing that song came from a few different things. When I was driving I liked to listen to country music because the stories would keep me awake. I remember a country song I heard — it was [about] an old couple kind of having breakfast and looking out the kitchen window. There's the old rusty play gym in the yard. They are reminiscing about how fast the time went by and all they have are the memories. So that was kind of the thought that went into the back of my head.

When Harry first started playing "Cat's in the Cradle," he would introduce it as, 'This song came from a poem my wife wrote when I wasn't home when Josh was born' — something to that effect. Actually, I always thought that was amusing because we always learn life's lessons too late. You don't know lessons about parenting when your first child is born or whatever. I'd learned the lesson when I first came to New York with my first husband and moved into his parents' apartment in Park Slope. I'm going out to teach every day. My husband is going to work as a lawyer. We're all home at dinnertime and his father has come home from work and he's trying to talk to his son. He called him Jimmy, and he said, 'You know, I'd like you to come down to the club' — being the local Democratic club — 'Come down to the club on Tuesday.' He's trying to engage him in his life. He wants to organize a career in politics for his son. He's very proud that his son had a law degree because he himself never went past the fifth grade. So he sees all this promise and possibility. He'd like to see his son be a judge someday; that to him is the highest level of accomplishment.

Anyway, there's no response. Nothing. No dialogue, no conversation. Nothing at all. So he started talking to me. He'd say to me, 'Will you tell Jimmy that' — this is while his son is right there in the room a few feet away — 'Would you tell Jimmy I'd like him to come down to the club on Tuesday,' and would start making appointments and dates through me sitting in the same room. So it occurred to me that they had no relationship. That if you don't form a relationship at two you're not going to be able to form one at whatever this was — 28. And they really didn't.

The song has had a tremendous impact. It's been used over and over again in Sunday sermons, and a lot on Father's Day, and books and articles; references in films and TV. The whole song is about paying attention.

I didn't have any intention of teaching a lesson. I was just telling a story because it was a story I saw that I felt very strongly about. I taught my kids folk songs. I was familiar with that kind of parable or whatever, and so it was just a story about what happens if you don't pay attention. But how could it be directed at Harry? As I say, the stories are learned after the fact. You couldn't direct it at Harry when he has his first child because he hasn't been there yet.

The song was written two years before Josh was born. It was written, as I say, at the time when he first went on the road. He'd come home — I was writing papers for my graduate program. I'd show him my papers. He'd put corrections on them, and it was one of a number of things that I was writing along with when I was doing *Make a Wish* stuff. It just happened to struck a chord after Josh was born. But it had already been there. It wasn't any comment on his parenting because it was before that. He may have directed it to himself, but I didn't.

**Thomas Downey (Friend; Former U.S. representative):** I met Harry through my friend Allard Lowenstein, who was a former member of Congress and an anti-war activist. I was running for Congress in 1974 ... and I was bemoaning the fact that I needed to be able to raise more money. (Allard) said, 'Well ... you should go see Harry Chapin, the singer-songwriter.' He said, 'Harry's like the prince of lost causes. He'll do concerts for anybody on the Democratic side.'

I want to say it was in the early summer of '74 that I went over to his house. He had a house in Huntington, not far from the water. Knocked on the door. It was about 8:30 in the morning on a Saturday. Harry answered the door in his underwear and said, 'Oh yeah! Yeah! Go sit on the porch!' It was a beautiful day.

So we were sitting there and he comes out with his guitar. He said, 'I want your reaction to this song.' So he plays for me "Cat's in the Cradle" and I sat and listened to it. I genuinely loved it. I said, 'That is a tremendous song. That's going to be a gigantic hit.' He said, 'Do you really think so?' I said, 'I do.' That's how I met him.

**Oscar Brand (Musician):** One day (Harry) said to me that he had decided to take one day off a week or at least a week during the month when he would be with the family. And right after he told me that — maybe two, three weeks — I saw him ... getting ready to take a plane.

I said, 'Where are you going?' He said, 'I have to do a show down south.' And I said, 'I thought we were going to be home at least a week every month.' And he said, 'That would be fine, but we do have to work, as you know.' And the next thing I knew, he had a song out which embodied that principle.

When he was getting ready to take the plane, he was sad because he could see that if somebody offered him a certain amount of money he would do that because he had to get his children to college. He had to give his wife money for the house to take care of everything.

**Patrick Leahy (Friend; U.S. senator):** I was still a state's attorney in Chittenden County. I was supposed to go down to a thing in Boston with the district attorney of Suffolk County that would be in the Boston area, have dinner with him that evening, and spend the night. So I left before our kids even got up — it was probably 4 o'clock in the morning. I'm driving ... and a Chicago station came in and they were playing "Cat's in the Cradle," which I hadn't heard. I didn't know Harry Chapin.

It just really resonated with me — so much so that I stopped at the dinner briefly that evening, cancelled my hotel room, got back in the car, and drove back to Burlington, Vermont so that I'd be in the house when the kids woke up in the morning. I'd have breakfast with them and drive them to school.

I probably got about three hours of sleep, but I've never forgotten that.

**Josh Chapin:** "Cat's in the Cradle" went to Number One in December 1974. I remember being in our kitchen and somebody kind of coming in and announcing that it had just gone Number One. There was some sort of hat that said "Number One" on it, and they put it on my dad.

**Jason Chapin (Son):** The fact that he was entered into the Grammy Hall of Fame for "Cat's in the Cradle"; the fact that he's still recognized for some of the things that he's done so many years after he died — it's really amazing.

"HELLO, HONEY, IT'S ME"

\* \* \*

## THE NIGHT THAT MADE AMERICA FAMOUS

**Ron Palmer (First guitarist):** "Cat's in the Cradle" was Number One two weeks in a row and the week after that I was gone. It was all because of the musical [*The Night That Made America Famous*] that Harry wanted to do.

I was ready. I'd had enough and I was ready to leave. At that time, I had some ambitions myself of doing things and going in another direction. So all together, it all boiled down to the fact that it was time for me to go.

**Big John Wallace (Bassist):** (Ron) was very upset about the Broadway show. "Cat's in the Cradle" had just gotten to Number One. Our price jumped from $2,500 a night, or whatever, to $7,500 a night and all these gigs started coming in. But Harry had this kind of bug up his ass to do Broadway. Right at the peak, he shuts everything down and goes to Broadway.

**Sandy Chapin:** Edgar Lansbury and Joe Beruh ... were the two guys who approached (Harry). This was when he was at his pinnacle of fame on top of "Cat's in the Cradle." They wanted to do a Broadway musical and they went ahead with the planning and so forth. Harry was to be in it. They had to look for a director. They had to raise money. Harry did fundraisers out in the Hamptons, and so forth and so on.

Somehow I think he really got led into the wrong direction for his music. He was really prodded into it and it was a very, very busy time in his career too. He was working hard at building the Performing Arts Foundation, and

World Hunger Year, and doing concerts in Europe — and somehow managed to do that too.

**Alexandra Borrie (Cast member, *The Night That Made America Famous*):** Like all shows, there were good and bad points. The show was sort of ill-conceived in that it really was a concert. The idea was that it be his songs and because he did story songs, somebody thought that they would probably translate onto stage with movement and some choreography and a little bit of more of a narrative than you get at a concert. So that's really all it was. There was no plot. There was no narrative. There were characters that lived within the songs, but not played out on stage with any kind of dialogue.

**Mercedes Ellington (Cast member, *The Night That Made America Famous*):** It was quite an experience because it was one of the first times that two different types of music entities came together. I mean Broadway at that time usually had a kind of strict format as being something from books or whatever. The era of the jukebox musical hadn't appeared. This was an incredible marriage of Broadway discipline combined with this kind of folk-rock singer and having his band actually on stage.

**Alexandra Borrie:** Harry is the soul of them. They were his songs and he delivered them the way they should be delivered. I didn't find it difficult at all, what we were doing. You know, I've done many Broadway shows. I was trained and all the singers were trained. It wasn't as if we were doing complicated harmonic work necessarily. It's hard for me to remember exactly what the musicality did entail, but it certainly wasn't terribly difficult.

**Jason Chapin:** It was very innovative. I remember that it was a musical and they played all of his songs but they also were using live video. They had a guy on stage who was shooting the performers while they are performing and then it was put on a screen. I remember it was a typical Broadway set but they were trying to use a lot of technology. I think my father was trying to use a lot of his filmmaking skills to make it visually memorable.

**Mercedes Ellington:** There was a lot of grit in Harry's presentations and we were encouraged to be very real about situations because they addressed real-life situations. It wasn't like this was fiction. Harry wrote about real things.

**Big John Wallace:** I remember one night. They were all looking down almost like a scene out of *The Producers*, you know, with like absolutely blank faces. I don't think they were sure what they were looking at.

**Jason Chapin:** It was only three weeks later, I think, that they closed the place, so it was kind of not a very long memory. It definitely had mixed reviews and limited success.

I also remember that there was a little bit of a struggle going on because my father had committed to doing it and it was very important to him. I think his band members were very annoyed with him because they wanted him to go back out on the road because "Cat's in the Cradle" had just become Number One. Everyone was thinking, 'This is when your music career can really take off; not a time to start another career.'

**From "Harry Chapin Brings Songs to Stage,"** *The New York Times* **– February 27, 1975:** *The people who put Mr. Chapin's* *disks in the Top 10 are probably the ones who will most enjoy the show, which is more like an animated record album than a musical. But animated it certainly is.*

*The show's pretentiousness tries very hard to be unpretentious, and it will probably be best liked by present devotees of Mr. Chapin, by people who like a nice sentimental little story and people impressed by flossy-colored lights. With luck there may well be enough of them.*

**Mercedes Ellington:** It was like a family setting. We were open to his dressing room. He would play music — people would be singing in the dressing room area. It was just totally friendly and very conducive to creating.

He would encourage other people to be creative in their choices in choreography. The camaraderie between the choreographer and him was great. I mean they understood each other. Everybody understood each other's strengths and weaknesses.

It's like a recipe for a dish. You have all of these ingredients and you put it together and you try to make it palatable and attractive so that people will eat it. I think that there was a good group of people together, but not necessarily at the right time for a so-called Broadway audience to appreciate it.

**Tom Chapin (Brother):** The Broadway show sucked really. It was all in the wrong hands. All the decisions that were made were wrong. It still was a fascinating time, but it really was bad. It didn't set up anybody in the best light in the material at all. So yeah, it was a mistake, but Harry's credo and the way he lived his life was: "When in doubt, do something." I remember him in talks saying,

'There's nothing so boring as being a rock star.' So let's do Broadway. He had this thing: 'I want to win the Nobel Peace Prize and I want to win a Grammy. I want to do it all.' He was a glutton in the best sense of the word. A glutton for life.

What happened was Harry — more and more after the reviews came out — would do a third act, which was the concert. So people would go away really happy because he'd stay there.

**Joseph Stern (Producer, *Chapin*; Conceiver, *Lies & Legends: The Musical Stories of Harry Chapin*):** The show didn't work, that was clear. And (Harry) was in it. It just didn't have his charm, which was really the juxtaposition of him coming out afterwards and sitting in a chair and singing. It was like, 'There's no comparison.'

When I saw the show — if I had walked out, then I would have never done (*Chapin*). It was when he came out and sit on a chair for 45 minutes and just sang songs that I said, 'That's the show. It's him.'

**Fred Kewley (First manager):** Harry had made a decision to stop doing the road so much and to do a Broadway show so he could make music, be on a stage, and then get home every night to Long Island rather than flying all over the country. That decision was being made as "Cat's in the Cradle" was climbing the charts, as I recall. He and I had some pretty heavy-duty conversations about it. That thing was out there and climbing the charts and obviously good things are going to be even getting better. That's when he decided to do this Broadway show, which I fought as much as I could fight.

**Alexandra Borrie:** From my observation, it was too simple, too unimaginative. It just lacked things all over the place, except for Harry and his orchestra and his singing. That was there. We really didn't need to be. I don't think we added anything to Harry's work.

**Fred Kewley:** Broadway is a big deal to a very small crowd. For him to do that was a shame when he had a Number One song about to be climbing. The sales were going through the roof and the record company's telling me this thing is huge. It's a real thrilling time, but right when he could have capitalized on it and increased his money from $10,000 a night say to $20,000, $30,000, $40,000; to do a Broadway show made no sense at all in terms of a career move.

But it was a personal move. It was something he felt he had to do to keep his wife and his family happy. He had to stop all the running he was doing in the previous years. So he did the Broadway show.

Parts of it were very good. It was a good way to see a Harry Chapin concert. It really wasn't a Broadway show for the blue-haired crowd. When it ended, we were able to go out there and do some big outdoor venues with 30,000 people. Those were good times, but it could have been a lot better if we had had the time to really cash in on "Cat's in the Cradle" in every respect, in terms of building a career and building a presence.

**Big John Wallace:** I think a little bit of that wave had passed by and it did cost him in the long run. But it was something he definitely wanted to do.

**Alexandra Borrie:** Whenever I am somewhere and Harry

comes on the air singing, I stop; I stand there; I listen. I like to pay him that little tribute.

\* \* \*

## GET ON WITH IT

**Ron Palmer:** They made the decision to bring in hired guns. I think I only played on two tracks on the whole [*Verities & Balderdash*] album. One of them was "Cat's in the Cradle" — I did the high harmonic parts on that — and the other one was "Six String Orchestra." John didn't play anything on the album, except for his voice.

I thought, 'Jesus, this is no good.' I mean we're going to

destroy the essence of the whole thing here. I had nothing to say about it because, as I said, we were busy on the road. But I just thought it was the wrong thing to do.

**Big John Wallace:** That was with Paul Leka and we were recording at Bridgeport Recorders, I think, in this kind of grimy neighborhood right in downtown Bridgeport, Connecticut. That was a fun time but also kind of a bizarre time.

Paul, his big hit was "Na Na Hey Hey Kiss Him Goodbye." He was a fun guy. He brought in the great studio guys from New York — Don Payne on bass, Allan Schwartzberg on drums, John Tropea [on guitar]. It was a more commercial sound ... but obviously it worked because "Cat's" was (Harry's) biggest hit.

**Ron Palmer:** As long as we recorded in L.A., according to our contract with Jac Holzman, the studio time was free. But Harry wanted to be closer to home. So that decision was made. We did have to pay for studio time. I mean I'd much rather have been recording in L.A. than Bridgeport, Connecticut, I can tell you that. But that's the way it goes.

Paul was fun to work with. I liked him a lot, but I thought that the essence of the group was the four of us and what we did in our performances. I personally did not like the idea of bringing in strings and layering everything and using up all 16 tracks two or three times each. I just did not think that was the way to go. That was just my opinion.

**Zizi Roberts (Friend; Backing vocalist, *Verities & Balderdash*):** (Harry) played me that song, "Cat's in the Cradle," and sometime shortly after that he said, 'I want you to come sing on the album.' The song that I sing on, I sang such a high note — "She Sings Songs Without Words." I had a C above high C at the end of that. On "Shooting Star," you can hear me in the echoes and I think for a moment or two I harmonize with John Wallace. He gave me solo pieces on two songs and then he's the one that decided "Angelic female vocals." He put that on the [*Verities & Balderdash*] album.

Harry did not smoke cigarettes. He didn't drink alcohol. He didn't smoke marijuana. He didn't do any drugs. But I did go in the car with him. I did whatever I needed to do in two trips to Connecticut. The first one Harry drove and, I'm telling you, my heart was in my throat with him behind the wheel because he ran every yellow light on [Route] 110 going across to wherever we were going to get to the highway.

**Harry Chapin (From** *The Tonight Show Starring Johnny Carson* **– September 9, 1975):** *The thing is that you really can't make up as good things as a writer that really happen to you. Like a song on the last album I wrote was about a truck crashing with 30,000 pounds of bananas in it and I remember — true story in Scranton, Pennsylvania — and ... I wrote a song about it because the old man sitting next to me as I was coming through Scranton on a Greyhound bus looked up to me and said — he had no teeth, I suddenly realized — he said, 'Can you just imagine all them mashed bananas?' You know, it was sort of a freaky concept so I wrote a song about it.... It's turned out to be sort of an underground classic. I mean it's played on a lot of the FM stations. It just never became an AM hit because it's a little too long.*

**Sandy Chapin:** "[30,000 Pounds of] Bananas" is actually serious. It was kind of a tone poem when he first used to do it. Steve would play the piano and he would perform it almost as a spoken word. Then he put music to it and people would laugh. He was writing this as a comment on numbers. I mean, God knows, it was mild back in those days, but nobody was an individual identity anymore. You were a Social Security code, and a credit card number, and a telephone number, and a statistic, statistic, statistic. So that was his comment on numbers, thinking that he was taking the humanity out. It was very serious and then people started laughing. Then the audiences turned it into the kind of nutty thing with the extra verses that it became.

**Howard Fields (Drummer):** I don't think (chart success) changed (Harry) that much except to have the knowledge that he had more power and more leeway to do better and bigger things outside of the musical arena. I think that's where he really started thinking about politics, after "Cat's in the Cradle" was a hit. He was playing for 3,000 to 5,000 people a night instead of a thousand, 1,500 people a night. His audience doubled and a good handful of cities went way beyond doubling. I think he realized that there was great potential there, and not just to play more concerts for more people.

I think he was larger than life when he was playing for a thousand people as when he was playing for 10,000. It was the same thing. It didn't matter. He was just so energized always.

**Marie "Peachie" Marsden (Friend):** He did have one thing. He got to the point where he could request no mysterious meats when they put food out for them backstage. He said, 'We're really big now — we request no mysterious meats!'

❊ ❊ ❊

**Big John Wallace:** Right from the first album, Steve [Chapin] was playing keyboards and being involved in the production. He wound up producing a few albums. He became very much involved in the arrangements too.

**Tom Chapin:** Harry was trying to write the best stuff he could write, but I don't think he ever did it the way that, say, [Bruce] Springsteen did it or some other people who are fully musicians all the time. He would write something and say, 'That's the record. Let's go record it. And meanwhile I'm doing World Hunger Year and I'm doing this and I'm doing that, I'm doing this' — you know, it's a different head. Yes, he wanted to be the biggest thing in the world, but he didn't.

**Howard Fields:** We actually did our first show March 31, '75 and the Broadway show was still on. It was a Monday night show, which on Broadway is a dark night. That was the Arie Crown Theater in Chicago.

At the first concert I was 24. That was the first time I ever set foot on stage in front of more than a couple of hundred people — well outside of the Broadway show. But it was sold out. I think it was about 3,500 seats. Chicago and Detroit were Harry's biggest towns. It was a night I'll never forget.

We did that one show, and then I think we came back and we found out the next day that the [Broadway] show was closing; that this would be the last week. But again, that wasn't the worst news to me because I was much more interested in touring around the country with a prominent pop artist. So they booked a couple more shows in April. It was an experimental basis for a short time after which we were told that this is it, you're in the band. It just peaked from there. An awful lot of concerts.

He started booking shows once that Broadway show was over. It just didn't stop until the very end.

**Jason Chapin:** A lot of times he would do a concert somewhere in another state and then he would fly home very late at night, and come home in the middle of the night. I would sometimes hear him come home, but then I would get up and go to school and he would still be asleep. Then he would go off to meetings and then leave for another concert.

I've got a theory about (Harry) and his calling. He was very much inspired by and very much enamored by people like Pete Seeger and Woody Guthrie. I think he felt that they were willing to go against sometimes conventional wisdom or against what would have been best for their career because they were passionate about their causes. Pete Seeger being blackballed — I think my father really respected him for that; that he wasn't a sellout; that he really had his convictions and he had his passions.

**Josh Chapin:** I think Mom realized that — like this was what he was shooting for his whole life. So she let him go on the ride for a few years. But two things were born out of that. 'You got to get involved in something.' You can't just be running around charming ladies and playing an extra song. You got to be about something. That happened as early as Point Lookout. There was a guy named Allard Lowenstein — he got involved with his campaign.

So that's how early that started, and he admitted that that was mostly at the behest of — and with the general nudge from — my mom.

The second thing was definitely, 'You got to be home a little bit more.' There's a contract — I think it's from '78 or something like that — that says, 'In December of '78, I will only do 10 concerts.' But yeah, my mom was always saying like, 'Listen, you can't just be all over the place. You got to put at least four days in a row or five days in a row at home.' It was definitely an ongoing thing.

Neither of them were like loud or fighters or anything like that.... It was not necessarily dramatic, or upsetting, or volatile in any way. But it was happening.

# CHAPTER 5

## *WHY*

**Harry Chapin (From a 1980 concert program):** *So here I was, a new career going strong, faced with the questions of what to do with it. All my brave words of the '60s about the social responsibility of successful people became bluffs to be called. I believe that success brings responsibility. It also does not bring immunity to the consequences of our quickening march toward oblivious. The bottom line is that all of us should be involved in our futures to create a world that our children will want to live in.*

*I met Father Bill Ayres in 1973, and after 15 months of meetings and planning sessions we founded World Hunger Year, a non-profit organization dedicated to giving a greater visibility to and higher priority for the solutions to mankind's greatest problem, world hunger.*

**Bill Ayres (Friend; Co-founder, WhyHunger):** In the beginning, I was the one who knew about hunger. I'd feed (Harry) books and after a while he started feeding me books. I mean he really got into it and he became very, very knowledgeable; very articulate; and a great spokesman.

He always was involved in humanitarian causes and helping various politicians that he agreed with get elected. But he never did hunger and poverty, to my knowledge. When I presented it to him and to Sandy, they both thought it was a great idea.

**Sandy Chapin (Wife):** Harry and Bill Ayres were going to organize a concert with the UN for Bangladesh. Somehow, along the way, Harry's education started to change — that one march on Washington doesn't change the world; one concert for Bangladesh doesn't solve poverty and hunger.

He met Frances Moore Lappé and was educated in the whole thing of you can't treat the symptom; you have to get to the root causes. You can't do charity — you have to create change, and so forth and so on. She really was responsible, I think, for bringing people into a new approach and a new realization.

**Bill Ayres:** We made a sort of pledge to spend the rest of our lives dealing with hunger and poverty in some form or other. His form, of course, was doing these wonderful concerts and raising money. Half of all his concerts went to causes, mostly hunger. Then in '75, we started this organization that we called WHY. I had suggested that because I had been influenced by the great Brazilian educator Paulo Freire, who said, 'You really need to ask the why questions.' "Why is there poverty?" "Why is there hunger in a world that can feed itself?" "Why is there hunger in the United States, the richest country in the world?" We figured that would be a great name except when you answered the phone, if you said 'WHY' it would sound like an Abbott and Costello routine. We needed an acronym.

The first two parts were easy — World Hunger — and then what do you do with the Y? That became Year.

When people asked (Harry), 'What year is world hunger?,' he'd say, 'Every year until we end hunger.'

**Thomas Downey (Friend; Former U.S. representative):** Literally he was in the kitchen when he thought of World Hunger Year.

**Fred Kewley (First manager):** I met a lot of people because of him. Harry was doing this thing with a lot of star people personalities — 'I'll do one for you if you do one for me.' So if you wanted to get people involved doing an event for him — for world hunger or whatever — then he would agree to do a concert for whatever it is they were trying to do.

**Bill Ayres:** I was doing the radio show for WPLJ. It was a rock and roll station; I was interviewing rock stars there. I came up with this idea of doing the Hungerthon — taking over a radio station for a whole day and bringing people on who were experts in the field, and then also bringing on artists who would sing and talk about the issue as well. We did three of them in New York. We did a couple in San Francisco. We did Philadelphia, Washington, Dallas, Detroit, a couple of other places over the next few years.

One of the people who was sort of saying this in the field of international hunger was Frances Moore Lappé. She had written a book called *Diet for a Small Planet*. Then she and her partner, Joe Collins, wanted to write a book called *Food First*. Harry helped to fund that. We had both of them on. We also had people on from Oxfam and the

Red Cross and all of the big agencies. But we also had people on from community-based organizations, as well as politicians. And musicians — people came on and sang. I remember Richie Havens coming on, and Peter Yarrow. A number of people that were Harry's friends would come on.

We'd stay up for 24 hours, but there was a little caveat in that because we would like start on Saturday morning, go until Sunday morning. It was 28 hours sometimes, 30, whatever. But a lot of times these stations would have some pre-recorded kind of public service show on Sunday morning, and they didn't want to preempt that stuff. We said, 'That's OK,' so we would take a nap. I mean we'd take a nap in the strangest places.

One time we did it in the closet; we'd just stretch out on the floor. It would take me like 10 minutes or so to kind of unwind. It took Harry 10 seconds and he'd be out like a light. And they come wake us up and we were laying on a floor so it's not comfortable, but you're so tired that you just go out. They wake us up and I'd be groggy, man. I'd say, 'Awww,' and Harry would be in the middle of a sentence. He would just start right over again and expected me to be awake, which of course I wasn't.

**Frances Moore Lappé (Friend; World hunger author):** The main memory I have of Harry is doing something that I'm now dreaming up to do again — a combo of speaking and music. I don't know how many concerts he did this way where he would donate the proceeds to *Food First*. Joe and I, we'd give a little rap about hunger and how it's possible to solve it. Honestly, at this point, I don't remember how many times we did that, but we felt totally on the same wavelength — building on people's sense of possibility that we can solve this problem not just on guilt. Then we also did radio interviews with Bill. So Joe and I were on the Radiothon; Harry was on the Radiothon.

It was kind of a network in those early years of people focused on world hunger in the New York area who did these things together. We had some sessions at our home in Hastings-on-Hudson. I guess it was the early days of what became World Hunger Year. Joe was there, our research associate was there, and we all lived in this big place. I do remember certainly our coming together and trying to figure things out together.

**Shelly Schultz (Booking agent):** If he was in Chicago, he promised somebody in New Mexico that he'd do a benefit the next night. Then we'd have to find him a date out of that benefit to at least help his financial situation because he'd go to New Mexico on his own dime; give them all the money; pay the commission; pay his guys and then you have to get him a real job the next night. So it was always that. It was a chore but he was a day job. He was everybody's day job. As a matter of fact, we used to call him our "day job." We had a lot of big acts, but Harry was the "day job."

I was an agent a long time before I got Harry and I used to say, 'I never knew these cities were out there.' In order to keep him out, he needed to be out. He would go on the road, get $7,500 for a show and give it to the charity. The whole thing. It was amazing, you know. And let us take our commission by the way. Everybody around him who worked for him got paid. Everything else he gave away.

**Frances Moore Lappé:** Passionate. Very warm, very approachable, not a know-it-all in the least. It wasn't like he was the big shot and we were this small fry just trying to get started. It was really like a partnership and [he] respected that we really had a lot to offer, especially since we were his junior and we were just starting ourselves in our own organization. I'm really impressed that he really did treat us as equals and gave us time. He could have just given the money to us but also he gave us airtime. And he really shared the stage with us.

**Patrick Leahy (Friend; U.S. senator):** I was new in the Senate on agriculture; interested in nutrition matters. They called me up and said, 'Hey, we got this singer, Harry Chapin, and he wants to talk about nutrition. I know you don't normally take time with celebrities but he's really...' — I said, 'No, I'd love to meet him.' Long story short, we hit it off very well.

He was amazing. I tell people that — 'Look, Harry gets nothing out of this. He just wants to feed hungry people.' He heard me say that I thought hunger was a moral issue. He certainly felt that way. Bill Ayres felt that way.

I was still getting used to being in the Senate and I was still learning. He would bring me all these statistics on hunger in America.... They were back within a day with statistics from across rural America, including my own state. There was no question hunger was an issue.

**Livingston Taylor (Musician):** What really struck me about him was that in person he was larger than life. He took up a lot of room. I found myself just feeling submerged in the enormity of his personality.

It was impossible not to pay attention to him. He had a

lot of charisma, and when I met him he very much radiated a real confidence. Just a confident guy who seemed very comfortable with his charisma and energy.

**Shelly Schultz:** He had the balls of a Brahman bull. He would pick up a phone and call anybody and ask for whatever he needed for his charity. He would never do that for his personal business. It was only about his charity. He was amazing.

**Fred Kewley:** I think Harry wasn't good at rationing his energy. He wouldn't say no to anybody. He just wouldn't say no to anything.

**Shelly Schultz:** We always talked about his career because he spent so much time on the road. We talked about what he wanted to do and then I did what I could do. I mean he was a handful as a client but he was such a decent, good guy. You just wanted to work hard for him.

## ON THE ROAD TO KINGDOM COME

**Fred Kewley:** (Harry) was writing songs on the way to the studio to record the next album. I mean he was just barely squeezing his career in. His career fizzled out because of that — because it's all about the songs; it's about the writing. You got to write things that people want. He wasn't spending any effort on the writing because he was so involved with all these other things.

**Sandy Chapin:** He wrote too much too fast. Usually it takes three to five years sometimes for a new album. He was coming out with an album once a year.

He always had more than they wanted and he was pushing for double albums, and they were saying, 'Uh-uh.' He was also starting to get involved with social issues and they didn't want to hear about that. They said he should concentrate on music. Also he was unmanageable. He went his own way, did his own thing, decided how to operate.

They couldn't pinhole what his music was. I think he was a folk-blues singer but because everything was rock he was trying to, I don't know, push himself more towards a rock sound. But it wasn't rock. It was hard really to put him in a category.

**Josh Chapin (Son):** To me, *Living Room Suite* is a country album and I think "Jenny" is a beautiful country song. *Dance Band on the Titanic* is more of a blues and kind of swing album. I just love listening to them as a whole.

**Nancy Heller (Friend):** If I had to pick one album that was so brilliant, it was *Dance Band on the Titanic*. It was Harry's *Sgt. Pepper*. I mean it was a brilliant album. Might have got bogged down in technical difficulties and some of the critics were kind of hard on it, but the critics were always hard on Harry. He got used to it almost after a while because it was just, 'Let's beat on Harry,' you know. But I think *Dance Band on the Titanic*, as a concept and as an album, was probably the one I turned to the most.

**Marie "Peachie" Marsden (Friend):** "Flowers Are Red" — a friend of his came home and said that his son got a report card and they told him he was not marching along with the rest of them but 'we'll have him marching by the end of the semester.' This was a little kid — not talking college — and it pissed him off to no end. And that's what he wrote. That's why he wrote songs like that, in protest of that happening. That children should just be able to do what they want and be creative and everything.

Somebody come up to him at a concert — a blind kid. I remember he waited a long time outside in the line to get in to see Harry, and Harry held his hands and said, 'You like my music?' He says, 'What's your favorite song?' And he says, '"Greyhound," I'm on that bus. I can see that.' Harry was very impressed with that.

"Corey's Coming" — he quotes [my husband] Zeke about the railroad. In the song it says, "You might wonder why a young man would work out here alone. Well the job pays enough to keep some flesh on my bones." Harry created this song about an old man that Zeke used to work with. It's beautiful.

**Terri Klausner (Performing artist):** "Tangled Up Puppet" — to this day when I hear that song or sing that song, or when I hear "Cat's in the Cradle," if I really go into my heart when I hear them or sing them, I can't do them without crying. There's just something so human and touching in the heart about them.

"Tangled Up Puppet," one of the lyrics in that is a mother singing to her daughter: "I'm a tangled up puppet, all gathered in your strings. I'm a butterfly in a spider's web fluttering my wings. And the more that I keep spinning out in knots, the more I see what used to be and the less of you I've got." It's a story of a mother singing to her daughter, watching her daughter grow up and how they used to play. Then she was the be-all and her end-all in her daughter's eyes until her daughter found other things and moved on. It became makeup and boys and her own life. The mother just reminds the daughter, 'Just don't forget I'm always here and will always be here, and you're the most beautiful woman I've ever seen.' Even saying it makes me cry. It's just a beautiful, beautiful story.

Harry really wrote some beautiful stuff.

**Patrick Leahy:** He and Sandy, in the summertime, wanted to come by our old farmhouse. A close friend of mine from my high school days and his wife are there with their daughter; same age as our daughter — was about 14 or 15 at the time — and they were very close friends. Harry said, 'You know, I got a new song. I haven't published it yet. Sandy wrote the lyrics.'

We were by candlelight with the windows open. We don't have air conditioning. This light summer breeze is coming through and you can hear an owl hooting in the woods. It was like a Walt Disney thing. He sang "Tangled Up Puppet," looking straight at these two teenage girls. They're just watching him in awe. The four parents — my wife and I and our two friends — we're standing there with tears rolling down our faces.

**Howard Fields (Drummer):** There were songs we really liked. Probably lesser known things. We really liked stuff like "The Mayor of Candor Lied"; that was from *On the Road to Kingdom Come*. We had a nice musical experience putting that song together. I liked the things that we felt were more musical. There was a song called "Odd Job Man," which was a nice little story.

We weren't that thrilled about playing "Taxi" for the 800th time, but we knew it was a great song. We liked the ones that we were a little more involved in because "Taxi" he had recorded with his original band. We liked things that we did together as a band.

My personal favorite of all his songs was something from the first album called "Any Old Kind of Day," so it wasn't just ones that I was involved in creating. I liked a lot of the stuff from the early albums. "Mr. Tanner" was always a very, very big song at our shows.

One of the songs from the last album that we all very much liked was "Story of a Life." Yeah, that last group of songs there were a couple of things. "Story of a Life." "I Miss America" was a very good song; he did a very good introduction to that. So those are just a handful of things that I think — not just speaking for myself — we all liked.

**Marie "Peachie" Marsden:** "Story of a Life," he wrote that on a plane. He got on the plane and they had turbulence and he got the barf bag out. I said, 'Why, are you going to throw up?' He said, 'No, I got a great idea for a song.' That's what he wrote on the barf bag, those words.

**Josh Chapin:** I don't think he gets a lot of credit for playing with genres enough. "Bummer" is like a funk song. That's not a song that jumps off that says, 'Wow, this is a great song.'

**Melanie Marsden (Friend):** [My brother] Billy was singing "Bummer" in kindergarten and it's a pretty heavy song.

**Josh Chapin:** It was mostly my dad's fault. He was not interested in being in the studio. Anybody will tell you that. He was in there and he was off to do something else and he didn't take care of himself. They had to do a lot of stuff with his voice — especially towards the later years — to cover it up because he was tired and he wasn't taking care of himself.

* * *

**Don Ruthig (Personal assistant):** Obviously, the high was the album *Verities & Balderdash*, with "Cat's in the Cradle." He came out with some decent albums after that, but it got to the point where his writing was almost like, 'I have to put out an album.' You kind of got the feeling that he would have been better if he'd kind of gone out and meditated on a mountain for a month and worked on his music alone. Being as active as he was, he fit it in.

**Shelly Schultz:** We both found ourselves on a plane to

L.A. I'm sitting in first class and Harry's in coach. He spent the entire trip walking up and down the aisle writing a tune. He had a pad of paper and a pencil, and he walked past me 65 times on that flight. We certainly talked to each other, but he was in the middle of writing a tune. I never asked him what the tune was, but when he got off the plane he said, 'I got it!'

**Bill Ayres:** I don't know if you ever saw him live. He far outperformed himself on the stage than he did in the studio. He was bored in the studio. I suggested to him one time that what we needed to do was get about 50 people to all sit on the floor in the studio because he had what he called the "Chapin living room effect." What that meant was no matter how big the audience was, he would create the feeling of intimacy. He called it sort of semi-intimacy, so that it was like you being in his living room. I said, 'Why don't we do that for recordings?' He said, 'That's a great idea.' But he never did it.

**Patrick Leahy:** Some stars are, 'Look at me — I'm a star!' Not Harry.

**Fred Kewley:** He was thrilled to be a star. He was thrilled to be recognizable and while he was that, he wore it like a common man. [If] he had a concert in some 20,000-seat person town, he'd drive into town and say, 'You guys know where the high school is? Where's the Harry Chapin concert?' He'd lean out the window himself and he would wave to everybody. He loved waking up in the morning being a guy with some power who could have an effect on people and who was recognizable. He could do a show and knock them down every time. He loved all of that. He was thrilled to be able to do that.

**Sandy Chapin:** Harry would make a point when he had a concert of going to a school early, trying to get into a pickup basketball game on a campus, and talk to guys about who their heroes were and what their dreams were — and trying to get a pulse on what people were thinking at that particular time.

**Josh Chapin:** Through this whole deal, he didn't like artists who were too precious about their stuff. It's about connecting with the audience. He was much more interested in being in concert, showing people things live, and writing the next song or finding the next story.

**Fred Kewley:** In later years when he's running around like crazy, he missed a flight to a huge concert. I think it was in St. Louis or someplace where it was like an outdoor thing with, I think, 20,000 or 30,000 people. He was the headliner. He called me and said, 'I missed the flight. I got another flight and I can get out here, but it won't arrive until so and so.'

So, long story short, I found a helicopter to get him from the airport to the concert. The audience is there waiting for Harry. He's not there. The announcer was keeping the crowd up-to-date as to what he was doing. Then he comes over the crowd with his helicopter and does a couple of circles around the crowd. The announcers are telling everybody that he's up in that thing. He came down and walked out and said, 'I've never been late, so I know you guys have been fantastic and you're waiting for me so I'm going to give you a four-hour show.' And he did. He gave them a huge, really well-done show. He turned a negative into a positive.

That's a show that that crowd could talk to you about today, I'll guarantee it.

**Harry Chapin (From** *The Tonight Show Starring Johnny Carson* **– August 10, 1977):** *Some people have songs — I have careers. I have to do concerts that are about three, three-and-a-half hours long to do the standard number of songs per concert.*

**Shelly Schultz:** He got there when he got there. I would say that 99 percent of the time his commitment to his business was correct. He never fucked over an audience by being late. But if he felt that he needed to do more than he should be doing on stage — normally because somebody in the audience wanted to hear something — he gave it to them. Nobody ever left. Then he stayed and signed autographs.

**Harry Chapin (From a December 5, 1980 speech):** *I have an annual meeting with my accountant. Sandy has given up going with me because she always knows what they're going to say. They always say, 'Harry, there's good news and there's bad news. The good news is that you've made more money this year than ever before. The bad news is you ain't keeping it.'*

# CHAPTER 6

## *CHANGES*

**Fred Kewley (First manager):** I think Harry was a good man. He dumped me as his manager and that was devastating to me... because it was my first artist — could have been my last — and was my only means of making things work.

At the time I had no idea what kind of residual income I might have coming from it or what else might happen. I just didn't. I had a partner who managed [Kris] Kristofferson and I managed Harry, and he and I together were starting to manage some other people. I had that going for me, which probably saved my bacon.

That was it. No more conversations.

Harry was my first one. I tell people that he and I put each other in business.

**Ken Kragen (Second manager):** The only time in my management career that I ever worked for anybody else was in the mid-'70s. Probably about 1977, I was working for Jerry Weintraub, a very famous manager. He produced *Ocean's Eleven*; a lot of other movies. At the time he had

John Denver, Neil Diamond — we used to call it the "Four Ds." I remember Bob Dylan. In any event he decided to sign a "C," which was Chapin. And he sent me to meet Harry in, of all places, Canada.

It's seared in my memory because I arrived at the hotel and Harry was there in the lobby. I think he had already checked in and we went up, left my bags in the room after I checked in, and then went back out in the street. I found despite the fact that I was 6'2" and a pretty fast walker I couldn't keep up with Harry. I almost had to run next to Harry. He was always in a hurry going to everything. My very first impression of Harry was, 'Boy, you're going to have to run to keep up with this guy.' It was true because he was just doing a hundred things at once — flying from one end of the country to the next and then back, and doing concerts and charity work and all kinds of stuff.

We got to be very friendly and worked together. Then I left that company not long afterwards — maybe a year later or less. Harry decided to come with me.

**Sandy Chapin (Wife):** The person who really was the most helpful and most congenial was Ken Kragen because he understood Harry. He instituted the idea that after every concert Harry would sell materials, and sign autographs, and raise money so that — this is after he started World Hunger Year — every night he was working he could be making money.

**Ken Kragen:** It was a technique I had learned and done quite a bit — to get him to give — in his case, I think he gave all the money from his merchandising sales to charity. He would tell people as he was finishing a show, 'Follow me out to the lobby. I'll be out there as long as it takes. I'll sign anything you buy; the proceeds all go to World Hunger Year,' or one of the other charities that he was supporting. Then he'd just stay there. The fans were madly devoted to him and he made a memorable impression on all of them.

I had influence on how we raised money for charity, but I didn't have the kind of stature that I gained in the mid-'80s, you know, from "We Are the World" and "Hands Across America"; all the other projects I've done since. I was a mildly successful personal manager heading towards big success in the '80s with huge clients who were dominating the record charts. But by the time I really got to have the kind of leverage that I could have in a kind of Washington presence which I had for a while, Harry was gone.

**Sandy Chapin:** We both read *Jonathan Livingston Seagull*. Harry used to talk about example and so I would use *Jonathan Livingston Seagull*. I said, 'You can't just go around telling people to fly; you have to bring them along.' It was this whole existential conversation that we used to have.

**Ken Kragen:** He tended to say yes to everybody. It was a sort of Harry Chapin quality that if you needed him for something, he was just that great guy. I mean we had to kind of almost prevent him from doing too much. He would just try to do every single event; every single thing that anybody ever asked.

He was on the go, in this rush, which I later came to feel had a lot to do with his thoughts that he wasn't going to live past 33 or 34 at the latest.

**Patrick Leahy (Friend; U.S. senator):** He had an infectious smile and he'd just come bounding in. But if a 5-year-old kid wanted to shake his hand, he'd come to a screeching halt and shake his hand. You had to like him almost immediately.

* * *

**Jen Chapin (Daughter):** It's not like he was partying. He just had too many things he wanted to do. He absolutely wanted to be there for his family, but he absolutely wanted to make a difference in legislation. I have an image of there being an old-fashioned calendar with concert dates and it would say like "Greek Theatre: 5,000 people." There would be a number associated with how many people were going to be there and the capacity of the hall.

It was absolutely for validation purposes. He wanted to be able to please people and he needed to know that he was pleasing people. It's classic psychology.

**Byron Dorgan (Friend; Former U.S. senator):** Bruce Springsteen talks about Harry and what he meant and so on, and then he said Harry told him, 'I do one concert for me and one concert for the other guy.' That was what he did. I mean he really literally donated about half of his concerts each year to fight world hunger, which is very unusual for entertainers to do.

**Don Ruthig (Personal assistant):** I think that there was a certain amount of guilt about sitting on the stage and making a lot of money and it may have been that guilt that was somewhat of a driver for him. He felt that he had to give back and he felt it very strongly. It was kind of like making all this money wasn't quite legitimate.

**Howard Fields (Drummer):** Nobody got fired. Only one of us quit.

**Shelly Schultz (Booking agent):** 'Stay out of a city,' we'd say to him. 'You can't go back there. You were there seven months ago.' He says, 'I got to go back there. I got to do this thing.' So he suffered. We couldn't go back there for two years afterwards just to keep a little distance. You overplay something and you become like furniture in a city. Those are the things he never understood that you couldn't explain to him. And that he was not interested in. He never thought about those things.

**Don Ruthig:** We did a concert in Syracuse, New York one time. I was doing the sound for that and I had family up there. We're all sitting there waiting for Harry to show up. He came in about an hour late — it was some kind of screw up in transportation. He missed his flight or something like that. But here was an audience sitting there for an 8 o'clock show; it's 9 o'clock, and Harry is just arriving. Within five minutes they were all loving him. Everything was forgiven.

So many performers would get up and they would do their shtick; deliver a good concert; deliver the music; but didn't really connect. Their banter between songs was stuff that you could tell was kind of scripted. Not Harry. He could just come off the top of his head and relate to the audience and make it all better.

I remember Hampton Beach, New Hampshire one time.

He was like two hours late. He got into a cab in Boston and he told the guy he wanted to go to Hampton Beach. Somehow or other, he ended up circling Boston for like two hours before he finally got up there. He walked into this hall and he made it all better. It was just the way he could kind of meet people one-on-one within a crowd.

**Howard Fields:** We never did three-month tours. We were always out on the road for 10 days and home for three weeks; out for two weeks and home for five days; out for seven days and home for three days. It was like that, but the excitement was always there. You always wanted to do a good show and you always had a sense people were there for you. They are paying their hard-earned money to come hear these songs. So that was always there, that excitement and responsibility. But there was a certain monotony to it at a certain point.

**Shelly Schultz:** Everybody around Harry was fabulous. There was no stress around Harry other than Harry. Harry was stress but he didn't give it to anybody.

**Patrick Leahy:** He had a concert at Georgetown University once. We had had a bite to eat at the Senate Dining Room late in the day.... [My wife] Marcelle said, 'Look, I'll drive you to the concert, Harry. Patrick can catch up with us.' So she starts up — half the streets were blocked by construction so she was getting really nervous. She was going around these streets — 'Oh my God, I'm going to be late for his concert!' He finally turned to her and said, 'Marcelle, don't worry, I'm the star. They don't start 'til I get there.'

**Big John Wallace (Bassist):** He gave us plenty of rope, that's for sure.

One thing he used to annoy Doug [Walker] and me a lot with was when he was trying to get the crowd going — 'ARE YOU READY?' and all this kind of stuff. You know, the screaming, and the shouting, and the 10-minute introductions for five-minute songs.

One night it was really bad. Doug and I are in the bathroom after the show washing up and I'm going, 'Fucking Harry, man. ARE YOUR READY? ARE YOU READY? Shut the fuck up! I'm so sick of this shit!' You know how sometimes you have a feeling that there's somebody around — but I mean there was nobody in the stall. So I'm mumbling and pissing and moaning and all this stuff. Doug's just trying to calm me down.

The next night we're up on stage and Harry's going, 'ARE YOU READY? ARE YOU READY?' Screaming at the top of his lungs. He turns around; he gives me like this sly grin. He's looking right at me and he goes, 'Are you ready, John?' Well it turns out — he told us later — he was in the bathroom. He was taking a dump, and all of a sudden I come in and I'm screaming. He was like so embarrassed that he didn't want us to know he was in there. So he pulled his feet up and hid until we left. He never said anything except on stage.

**Tom Chapin (Brother):** It was Bridgeport, Connecticut. I do a set and it's not going over great, you know. It's OK. Usually it went over fabulously. When it was wonderful, it was a really nice thing, but the crowd was sort of a restive crowd. So I get off and Harry's not there yet. I finish my set and I go off and the promoter is frantic, 'No, you got to go back out there.' So I go back out and do three more songs and the audience is really shitty. I come off and I say, 'What the fuck is he doing?' Harry comes in all fired up — 'How's it going?' I grabbed him. I said, 'You know what, I can't fucking take this and I'm out of here,' and I stormed off.

I got in the car and they go do the show. I drive about halfway back to New York. I pull off and call my wife — you know, no cell phones in those days — so I pull off and it's a pay phone. I said, 'Bonnie I did this and I quit.' She said, 'You did what?' And I'm sitting there talking to her, and I said, 'I'm blaming Harry for this. This is not Harry's fault. This is my fault. I put myself in this place. I don't need to be here. I'm not doing this anymore.' She said, 'What?' 'I'm going back.' She said, 'What?'

So I get back in the car and I turn around and I go back. I get back just before "Circle," which is the way we end. I walk out and grab a guitar. Harry looks at me and off the mike he goes, 'I love you.' And then we sing "Circle." Then we come back off and Harry's out signing.

John Wallace goes, 'Tom, ugh, that was such a dramatic exit; you ruined your exit. What did you come back for?' They were all laughing at me.

Then Harry came back and I said, 'Harry, I can't do this anymore. It's driving me nuts. I'm just going to end up hating you and blaming you for this. So what I'm going to do is finish this tour another month-and-a-half and then I'm going to just do my own thing.' He said, 'Really? Well I really want you out there.' I said, 'I know you do, but I'm just telling you it's not working for me and I want to not be blaming you. I love you.' He totally got it. Anyway, we were always clear about it from then on, which was great.

**Big John Wallace:** The way I remember it, (Tom) stayed about seven months and then he was gone. He's always had more of a competitive issue with Harry, I think, than Steve. Steve's relationship is different. Steve knows how good he is, and the brothers know how good he is and how valuable he is. So he didn't really compete with Harry where Tom did, in a sense, because he is more of a frontman. Not that there was any problems or anything, but I think that Tom just figured he was ready to go his own way.

**Tom Chapin:** It was hard to be in this orbit if you were a brother. Steve had a lot of trouble with that. And the band got angry at stuff. When I was doing the benefit stuff that was great; it worked out great. We did a couple of tours. Went to Europe together at one point with the whole family and he and I did all the air bases in Germany and France. It was really fun. I always had the chance to do my own stuff anyway.

**Jen Chapin:** (Steve's) the most trained and widely capable. I think Harry really depended on him. He used Steve to sort of fill in for his own insecurities.

**Tom Chapin:** Steve was always a behind the scenes kind of producer, that kind of thing, and was not as comfortable at being the lead dog. I'm very much like Harry. I'm comfortable being on stage telling you about my world. So he and I understood each other really well in that way.

**Marie "Peachie" Marsden (Friend):** Steve wrote all the parts for every instrument. He was brilliant. Harry would just strum it; figure it out; say, 'Close enough for Chapin music.' Steve would just look at him and shake his head. Steve was the perfectionist.

**Howard Fields:** Tim Scott was the first cellist. When I joined the band, the second cellist was a fella named Michael Masters. Michael Masters left the band and we had an interim guy who didn't work out. He was with us about six months and his replacement was Kim Scholes. When I think of the band — the five of us playing Frisbee and softball — he was the guy; he was our cellist. The five of us — Steve Chapin, John Wallace, Doug Walker, Kim Scholes, and myself — that was the band. Those were the golden days, the five of us together. But Kim succumbed to certain pressures that we were all feeling at a certain period in the life of the band and Harry's career and he just didn't want to do it anymore. So he took off.

Kim was the only one who quit. It was a moment of haste. In the middle of a concert, he just left the stage. That's just something that occurs to me when we're talking about the difficulties of getting along with (Harry). But it was not just the difficulty of getting along with Harry as the difficulty of getting along with any employer. It's kind of stressful in a pressurized situation, having to be on the road for long periods of time, day after day, and things aren't going well. If they don't go well over a period of time, it's just stressful. We all felt it, but Kim just didn't want it anymore.

**Big John Wallace:** In a very dramatic fashion [Kim quit] by slowly taking his keyboard stack and just pushing it forward until it just fell over. Then he walked off. Very dramatic. But that was the exception. I mean you can maybe be annoyed at each other or something every now and then just like anything else, but there were never really any big fights. I mean Harry never got in a fight with anybody. He was always round-shouldered and goal-oriented. He hated conflict and fighting and he would always try to straighten things out. He was very cerebral. Reason over emotion. Doug and I — like every six weeks we would have a fight, but it was nothing.

Tim Scott was in for two years, and then Mike Masters came in for at least three-and-a-half maybe. And then for nine months, Ron Evanuik. Ron came before Kim. Then Kim. And then the last one was Yvonne Cable.

I liked Ron. By the way, he was a great bass player too. I mean he could play some Jaco Pastorius, the late great bass player. I mean I was amazed watching Ron Evanuik play a couple of those tunes note-for-note like "Portrait of Tracy," which is all harmonics and stuff. He was real good. But as a cellist, probably he wasn't as strong, you know, and I think he just decided to go in another direction. Of course Kim was a high-level cellist.

**Howard Fields:** He'd commit the band to doing benefits and we didn't care that much about doing benefits. What we did care was doing quality concerts. That was our big picture, and Harry's big picture might have been: 'We have to do this show. We have to get this money for this organization.'

Harry had us do a show out in Texas on Tuesday, so obviously a sound company can't get there. You have to hire backline — the equipment, drums, keyboards, amplifiers. On this particular night, Kim played a little keyboards on a couple of songs and the equipment he had was inferior. I'm not telling you anything that wasn't documented by saying that. He just kind of like pushed the keyboard onto the floor and left the stage and left the band that night. So that's why it was Harry's sometimes lack of vision about putting on a quality show. His point was: 'We got to do it. We got to get this money for this,' whatever it was. And we said, 'Yeah, but what about putting on a good show? Wouldn't it be better to do that?' So that's where the rub was. That's a good example of some of the disagreements we had with him.

**Big John Wallace:** (Harry) was up front about it. Of course he did a zillion solo benefits. We averaged maybe 125 nights a year or something, and he did — I would say from '75 on — probably another 50 at least himself. But he asked us and we agreed to do 24 a year; two gigs a month for World Hunger Year. So we did that, and maybe some more, but I don't think anybody ever resented it. It was a good cause and how can you resent somebody when the leader is the hardest working guy. What are you going to say? I mean he's out there leading by example. He would never ask anybody to do more than he wouldn't do.

**Patrick Leahy:** Near Rutland, Vermont — the Killington Ski Area — they were doing a benefit for Fire and Rescue. They asked Harry if he would be willing to sing. Harry, before he went on, had a terrible cold. His voice was far more gravelly than usual. I said, 'Harry, you could have just bailed on this.' He said, 'No, these are good people. They need the money and I promised them.'

Then he went on the stage. Oh my God, I would give anything to have had a recording of that concert. You wouldn't know he had a cold or anything else. And he was doing it solo — no backup or anything.

**Don Ruthig:** It was kind of like herding cats a lot of the time. Yeah, he was very frenetic. I mean at that point I think he was doing something like 200 concerts a year. At least half of them were benefits. So he was all over the place. Then he got involved in all the lobbying efforts. So yeah, his schedule was nutso. As a matter of fact, I used to keep the official airline guide, the OAG, by my bedside because I could expect at night after a concert he'd call me and say, 'How do I get from here to there?' Usually he needed to be in Washington the next day to do some lobbying, or he needed to go someplace else. There was never a dull moment.

**Sandy Chapin:** I used to say to Harry, 'Well, you made this choice, I didn't.'

**Howard Fields:** It was pretty obvious to his inner circle — his band and his family — that that's where his future was. I don't know that he ever said anything, but it was pretty clear that he was using the Long Island community where he lived as a stepping stone into local politics. Who knows where it would have went from there.

**Sandy Chapin:** He was always afraid that he wouldn't be productive enough, so he would force himself into a vice. When he was raising money on Long Island, he would actually call a press conference and announce that he was going to do a fundraiser for the new Long Island Philharmonic and he was going to do it in Nassau Coliseum. He had no musicians; nothing lined up. He would set a date and then he would get on the phone and start to make it happen. He would force himself into the vice and announce something that no way was in place in order to force himself to have to pull it off.

**Marie "Peachie" Marsden:** 'When in doubt, do something,' he would always say. If you don't know what to do next, just do something.

# CHAPTER 7

## *"GAPIN' CHAPIN"*

**Bill Ayres (Friend; Co-founder, WhyHunger):** Harry kind of always called himself "Gapin' Chapin" because he wasn't afraid to sort of make a fool of himself. We'd go into a meeting and often we'd play good cop, bad cop. He would get up and yell at people and say, 'Hey, we got to do this. We got to do that.' I'd say, 'Well maybe we ought to just think about this.'

This one day we're walking into this meeting with the Council of Churches and there's all these religious leaders. I said to him, 'You got to be on your good behavior.' 'Don't worry about it.' I'd always sit next to him so I could kick him if he sort of went off. We walk in and he goes and sits between two other guys so I can't sit next to him, and he smiles at me. He had this big smile like, 'I got ya. You can't touch me.' He knew what he was doing exactly. We both laughed at each other.

**Jen Chapin (Daughter):** I was vocal — 'Daddy, why do you have to work on your birthday? Why do you have to work on my birthday? Why do you have to work on this holiday?' I think my mother said that it was me and Jono. Everybody else were sort of puppy dogs. Like they would take what they would get, but we would give him a hard time. I did it in a little girl way. Jono did it in a teenager way.

**Byron Dorgan (Friend; Former U.S. senator):** He was unpretentious. I remember the day I met him at Rutgers University, he was driving a little white Volkswagen. He said, 'I'll give you a ride.' I'm thinking, 'He's going to have a pretty big vehicle.' He's driving a little white Volkswagen.

❈ ❈ ❈

**Harry Chapin (From a 1980 concert program):** *A yearlong effort that began in 1977, by WHY, the Food Policy Center (our Washington-based lobbying organization), and myself, has resulted in the formation of a Presidential Commission on World Hunger. I have been appointed by President*

*[Jimmy] Carter to the Commission whose mandate is: why, after 20 years of programs and expenditures of billions of dollars, has there been no significant progress in dealing with the hunger problem?*

**Bill Ayres:** He would either charm (congressmen) or he'd bowl them over. In other words, he'd walk into a congressman's office — and I was with him on a lot of these — and say, 'You and I both know hunger is wrong. It's immoral. It's crazy. We don't have to have it. We need to have a policy to fight hunger around the world and here in the United States. Would you sign onto this Presidential Hunger Commission?' Most of them did. A lot of them did because they liked him and they believed in the cause. Some of them, I think, did it because they just wanted to get rid of him.

We'd walk the halls of Congress, and I'm a very fast walker, and he would leave me in the dust, man. He was fast. I have long legs and he had longer legs and we'd go around. I'd say, 'Hey slow down!' But when he'd get in the office he didn't slow down either, you know what I mean. He'd just go right at them. And he had some allies. I mean he got a number of people. On the Senate side we had Pat Leahy in Democrats and Bob Dole signed on. Then on the House side, we got Rick Nolan — I think he was from Minnesota — and Ben Gilman, a Republican from New York. They were sort of our key people in the House [of Representatives] and Senate.

**Thomas Downey (Friend; Former U.S. representative):** Harry had an inside flair in the Congress — he had me. We did this together. I mean I don't want to overstate my role here. It was much more advisory than anything else. But I introduced him to other members of Congress who were friends who both liked his music and agreed with his positions.

I took him down to the House gym once, which was really a terrible breach of protocol on my part. He was, along with his brother, a very good basketball player. I remember he was excited to be in the House gym, which was kind of an inner sanctum until he saw some member of Congress that he wanted to talk to. He was about to accost this person as they were getting dressed. I said, 'No, we don't talk to anybody at the gym.'

What we would do is we would basically set the meetings up and he would go to them. Sometimes I would accompany him and sometimes I wouldn't. He didn't need me to make kind of a forceful argument to my colleagues. It was not just his ability to basically sell the message, which was very important, but his ability to enthuse those who were going to be kind of the legislative warriors. That was also one of his constant skills.

**Byron Dorgan:** Harry was a breathless character. He talked. And when he was excited, he talked a lot.

**Robert Mrazek (Friend; Former U.S. representative):** Boy, he won over a lot of Republican members of Congress and senators. He would just come into a room and he projected this kind of aura. You could feel the goodness in him. Even cynical Washington politicians could feel that power and be moved by it.

**Patrick Leahy (Friend; U.S. senator):** I told him once that I read that you never want to have an alligator grab you because you have no way of prying their jaws apart. I said, 'Harry, I know you're walking down the hall. I'm about ready to hide under my desk because the alligator is going to grab me and not let me go until I say yes.' Of course, I didn't hide.

I would invite other senators to come by. We'd sit around the conference room and they'd have their picture taken with him and then they'd go to leave. I'd say, 'Harry, there are a couple of points you want to make, don't you?' One time he was literally blocking the door until he finished his points.

**Bill Ayres:** When we were in Detroit, we did a concert with James Taylor, Gordon Lightfoot, John Denver, and Harry. Just four guys on guitars; four guitars on a stage. We did it at Cobo Hall and raised — I remember this number — $156,000, which would be a lot of money today. In those days it was a tremendous amount of money. We used it to open an office in Washington to sort of be a shadow to this Presidential Hunger Commission.

**Gordon Lightfoot (Musician):** When we got there it was very well-staged, and promoted by CKLW, the big Top 40 station in the Detroit area.

There were about 13,000 or 14,000 people in there that night and the theater was set up in the round. We just had a lovely time. There's some lovely photographs of the four of us — John, and Harry, and myself, and James. Lots of chatter, and lots of laughing, and 'When can we do it again?'

It was done in a very simple manner. All of the performances were done solo. Terry Clements played lead guitar behind everybody because he's got a great ear. We chose a number by Bing Crosby to close the show for all four of us to sing.

❊ ❊ ❊

**Harry Chapin (From a December 5, 1980 speech):** *I think the reason I'm involved in hunger is because I think it's absolutely obscene in a society that could feed every human being six times over, in the United States of America—which is the richest, most vibrant society in the world—that we have 20 million Americans chronically malnourished. That, to me, makes my success a mockery.*

**Walter Falcon (Member, Presidential Commission on World Hunger):** Harry cared deeply about food and agriculture and hunger. He and I saw the world somewhat differently as to what was needed to fix the world and so we were sometimes on the same side of the fence, sometimes on opposite sides of the fence. But our conversations were cordial and lively.

**Big John Wallace (Bassist):** Ever since '75 on, he was

spending a lot of time in Washington, making a lot of friends and having a fair amount of influence.

He was proud of this. There was one 17-day stretch when he was doing his heavy lobbying for a Commission on Hunger and he said, 'In 17 days, I haven't laid down in a bed.' He would get the last flight out after the gig; he'd sleep on the plane; he'd spend all day in Washington; he'd sleep in the cabs; sleep on the plane back to the gig; do the gig. Seventeen days in a row. He was very, very physically fit and a dynamo.

**Bill Ayres:** Harry called me up and said that, 'Hey, we're going to the White House. We're going to meet with the president's son, and hopefully the president, and what we want to do is to do a concert.' ... The president got this idea of doing this concert for Africa. So he called us and Harry said, 'You got to get dressed up.' I said, 'What do you mean, me get dressed up? You got to get dressed up. You don't have a suit.' He said, 'Oh yeah I do. Sandy just took me out and got me a suit at this store in Huntington.'

I meet him at the plane over at LaGuardia Airport and we're standing on line. He bends down to pick something up and 'KRRRSSHH,' the whole thing rips. I mean it didn't just rip; I mean it ripped. The pants were too tight for him, obviously. He had a big hole down the back of his pants and he showed me that.... So we get on the plane and I said, 'We got to get this fixed.' He said, 'Yeah,' but then the plane got delayed. We wanted to make the meeting. So he had a newspaper and he held the newspaper right behind his rear end with his left hand and he went around and he shook hands with people, holding the paper next to his rear end. After doing this for a while, he said — as only Harry could — 'Well this is ridiculous. I've been peddling my rear end for hunger all over the country, but this is silly.' He turns around and he shows everybody and the guys all laugh. It was a room full of record company executives and government officials and they all thought that was wonderful. He hadn't met [Jimmy] Carter yet. We met a couple of his sons that day.

At first, he decided he would cover it up because I said to him, 'I hope you're wearing underpants.' He said, 'Yeah, I'm wearing underpants, don't worry.' But it was hysterical. I told that story at his funeral, actually.

**Don Ruthig (Personal assistant):** Thank God we didn't have cell phones then; the man would never have rested. He would have had the world's highest cell phone bill. But there were times when it was just a good time, a good buffer zone for him.

The other thing is that we could leave for LaGuardia with 45 minutes before a flight and he'd make the damn flight even though it was a half hour drive. He didn't have to worry about parking the car or any of that nonsense. There were times when he drove himself and parked the car under a bridge. The car would get towed because he was in so much of a hurry. He'd just park it wherever and leave it.

Most of the time he would fit the lobbying effort in-between gigs. He'd be out in Detroit doing a concert and first thing in the morning he'd catch a flight to Washington, spend the day there, and then be back out to Chicago that night. He did that a lot, where he would just fly in, do his business, and fly out again. That's when I would get these midnight calls: 'I got to get to Washington tomorrow. How can I get there?' I'd find him a flight and get him in there.

There was a flight — he wrote a song about it — called Northwest 222 and that flight, I think, originated in Minneapolis, hit Chicago, Detroit, and then JFK. It came in at about 6 o'clock in the morning. Harry was practically a resident on that flight.

I think he was pretty well-known within the airlines. He'd call me — 'I'm on Northwest 222; meet me at Kennedy.' It came in at like ... 6:30 in the morning. 'Ugh, Harry, please. Give me a break.' But I'd meet him.

**Bill Ayres:** One great story is that Harry's down in Washington and he's riding with Pat Leahy and another senator and they are going to go into the Capitol. They are in a car with somebody driving the car, and the guard stops them. Leahy says, 'I'm Senator Leahy,' and the other guy said, 'I'm Senator so and so.' He said, 'Well can I see your passes,' and they both look and say, 'Oh gee, we left them.' The guy said, 'I'm sorry, I can't let you in.' And then he looks back and he said, 'Oh, are you Harry Chapin?' And Harry said, 'Yeah.' 'Oh, go on in.' And Harry rubbed it in. He loved that story. Told that story all the time.

**Patrick Leahy:** Right behind me was Harry, and one of the guys said, 'Oh, Harry Chapin, so great to see you! Go right on in, sir; they're waiting for you!' I'm like, 'All right — put me in my place...'

Security (was) nowhere near what it is today.

**Ken Kragen (Second manager):** He finally got [President] Carter to sign to create this committee that he had been lobbying for forever. He was very close friends with Patrick Leahy. Harry is at the White House and the president is signing the bill. Harry is still selling him on why he should be doing this. Pat finally leans over and taps Harry on the shoulder and says, 'Harry, he's signing it. You can quit selling him now,' which we thought was very funny.

**Patrick Leahy:** We did this in the Cabinet Room of the White House. We go in and there's Bob Dole and myself, several others, and Harry. Harry starts in with, 'Mr. President, you gotta do this.' 'Well, I think that's a good idea.' 'No, Mr. President, you also gotta blah blah blah.' 'Well, I think it's a good idea.' 'No, and another thing, Mr. President!' Finally, Bob Dole and I both said, 'Harry, hush up. Don't talk about it. You won him over!'

Jimmy loved it.

**Dave Marsh (Friend; Music critic):** Ralph Nader called [*Rolling Stone* Editor-in-Chief] Jann Wenner and said, 'You should send someone down because Harry Chapin is the most effective outsider I've seen on Capitol Hill.' By that time they already created World Hunger Year. That was the first time I reported about him.

**From "Singing for the World's Supper,"** *Rolling Stone* **– April 6, 1978:** *"It's gotten so bad,"* Carter concluded, *"that even [my daughter] Amy is asking me what I'm going to do about world hunger." And then, in a voice so low his audience couldn't be sure they'd heard him right, "I think it's a good idea." Chapin had pulled it off.*

**Patrick Leahy:** The meeting was very good. (Carter) did the Hunger Commission. He put money for feeding programs in the Presidential budget. Because we had people like Bob Dole and myself and people across the political spectrum in both parties, we almost got it through.

**Walter Falcon:** As I understand it, the [Presidential World Hunger] Commission was supposed to look at the issue of hunger both abroad and at home and to make recommendations as to what the United States — and to a degree the federal government — might do to improve things.

The composition of the Commission was somewhat unusual. In retrospect, it probably wasn't the strongest group that could have been put together on world hunger issues. There were many different backgrounds represented; lots of different points of view. It was hard for the Commission to reach closure on some of the issues and that's why when you look at the report, there seems to me to be an awful lot of footnotes, reservations, and so on.

You would experience someone who was not shy; who was very energetic; who you could tell felt deeply about the subject. But I didn't think Harry was wonderfully well-informed, or perhaps even well-staffed on some of the bigger issues, which, in fact, turned out to be the important ones now with the benefit of history.

**Bill Ayres:** Was the Presidential Hunger Commission successful? Yes, it was, in the sense that it finished its work and it published all these findings, which — if Carter would have been president — he would have put into effect. At least I hope he would have. But most of them did not get put into effect because [Ronald] Reagan won.

It was a heartbreaker. But a lot of people got influenced by it and some very interesting pieces of legislation and policy came as a result of it, even though it didn't take room in the way we hoped it would.

**Walter Falcon:** The March 1980 report of the Presidential Commission on World Hunger has a title of *Overcoming World Hunger: The Challenge Ahead*. It is 250 pages. It came just at the end of the Carter administration and I don't think it had very much impact, frankly. But as a historical piece, it's quite interesting.

As I remember it, we tried desperately to finish the report before Carter left office. Whatever the intention was, Carter has a deep and lasting interest in hunger and agricultural development.

It's not a bad report; it just sort of fell between the cracks between administrations. Reagan was really on to different things. Carter was lame duck on recommendations.

**Ken Kragen:** One of the true stories that happened with (Harry) was that I had taken him to a Laker game on the night of the midterm elections.... He had been sitting there at the Laker game — they were actually flashing the results of the election up on the screen. The Republicans were sweeping into power — it was during the Reagan administration. In any event, all I know is Harry turned to me and he said, 'I've got to get to a plane. I've got to get back to Washington.' He actually got up and left in the middle of the game. He said, 'The Republicans have run on this idea of saving the economy, helping the economy, spending less and stuff, and I can show them how curing poverty in this country will reduce crime. They have run on an anti-crime platform and I can show them how, if we can reduce poverty, I can make this ideal.'

He was watching the people he had supported one-by-one go down in defeat and yet he had turned it immediately into: "This is a terrific opportunity."

**Bill Ayres:** One of the defining moments I guess was a negative one, when he and I sat and watched the results of the Reagan victory. We looked at each other, and we said, 'We just worked our asses off for three years and it looks like it's all going to go down the drain now.' After sitting in that vein for like half an hour or so, we both said, 'OK, what do we do now?'

**Thomas Downey:** I would not have expected Reagan to be very much help to us on this stuff. I mean it was his administration that wanted to consider ketchup a vegetable for purposes of the school lunch program, which was a big joke at the time.

**Walter Falcon:** Everybody just thought it was over. I don't recall it much as Reagan nixing it, as opposed to the Commission had sort of done its thing and it was over. We had done our task; the report was over; we were having trouble getting some closure on a lot of the key issues; and the Commission finished. The Commission died naturally rather than having been murdered from the outside by somebody else.

**Jono Chapin (Son):** That probably was his greatest frustration was dealing with bureaucracies, red tape, the status quo — 'No we can't do this because it's going to require a little more work from somebody.' That sort of pushing up against the brick wall and knowing that, 'Boy, it's going to take quite a bit to change this,' and recognizing that you certainly can't do it alone so you need to rally some others. That probably was his greatest gift. I think the music ultimately served him well because it was a conduit to achieve some of those other deep-seeded needs to make a difference.

**Howard Fields (Drummer):** [Harry was] a lot more disappointed than when that Broadway show closed, I can tell you that. Very, very disappointed when Carter lost the election. You saw it on his face.

It was a big lesson to him. I mean I have little doubt that he would have gone into politics. Might have been Senator Chapin by now.

# CHAPTER 8

## *THE ROCK*

**Howard Fields (Drummer):** Whenever (Harry) wasn't doing something tied to his music career; or tied to his political life; or tied to his benefit life, all the time that was left over he would be home.

**Gordon Lightfoot (Musician):** Harry had a large family and he cared about his family a lot. You know, his being on the road; he tried to keep everything down to a dull roar. It was tough. I know I could never do it 100 percent. I paid for it too as time went by.

**Don Ruthig (Personal assistant):** Harry used to get himself in trouble because he would know that he wasn't spending enough time with his family because he was out on the road or whatever. I think (Sandy) would get kind of on his case a little bit about it, and then he would make this commitment: 'OK, Sandy, I'm not going to take any more gigs. I'm going to take this month off.' That would last for about three days. So while he knew that he needed to spend more time with his family, there was always something else that needed to be done. There was always something that came up that kind of took him away from it.

**Shelly Schultz (Booking agent):** I don't know this for sure, but I think Sandy probably had a tough way to go with him. He was not attentive. He was always on the road.

**Big John Wallace (Bassist):** Let's just say I think it involved a little address book. The way I remember it, an address book was found that had 73 names in it. I think things started going downhill from there.

**Sandy Chapin (Wife):** There definitely was some kind of black book address book. That's part of the life that Harry lived on the road.

**Zizi Roberts (Friend; Backing vocalist, *Verities & Balderdash*):** There was one night when he was out. Sandy was not letting him back in the house. That was like right after the black book. She was upset with him. I want to say we had come back from the studio and Harry says, 'I need a place to crash tonight.' So we put him in the house where we were all living.

He knew that I knew. Of course he knew that I knew.

**Jason Chapin (Son):** There was definitely a time where my mother found out about his infidelities and she kicked him out of the house. He had to win her back and he had to make amends with his family. I think at that time ... he needed to make a deal with her where if he was playing in some place like Chicago, he had to fly home to be home for the night, and then he needed to fly back to Chicago, or wherever, for the next show the next night. She just felt that he couldn't always do what he thought what made sense — that she needed him to be a husband and a father and to make the commitment to his family.

**Josh Chapin (Son):** I can pretty much guarantee that he stepped out of the relationship. It was just a reality of his ego [and] his insecurity of what he needed to be fed when he was younger. My mom was very conscious of it. One of the reasons that he was able to communicate with so many people in such an intense level and such an intimate level was because he was flawed. He knew he was flawed. He would admit to you that he was flawed.

**Jono Chapin (Son):** The other thing that happened with Harry is you sort of got snippets, you know what I mean. We had concentrated time when we had fantastic opportunities to go on extended trips to Europe and Australia and different places around the world. But then there were periods during the school year where he was off doing concerts. When he might be around, you could be in school or when he was around, it was kind of like, 'All right! Hey everybody, jump in the car. We're going to a movie.' Or going out to dinner, and then going out to a movie. It was kind of like a pretty big hit and run. You know, 'Here it is. This is what we're doing; this is the game plan.' It's a different way of life.

I certainly sort of adjusted to it and rolled with it and I think it's just the way you grow up. You kind of adapt to things. So it's funny because when I sort of operate that way with other people, it can throw them.

**Jason Chapin:** When we moved to Huntington, there was more going on all the time. We had this music room in the house where he would go in and either listen to music, or he would write lyrics, or he would be working on some other non-music project. There was always something going on. A lot of times when he was away it was pretty normal around the house. We had our routines with school, with sports, and friends, and family. Then when he came home it was like a mini hurricane. There was always somebody coming by to meet with him or he was on the phone with somebody. We would go out to dinner and we'd go out to the movies and he would try and do the normal family things, but when we did it with him, it was a little different because somebody would recognize him.

**Harry Chapin (From an unedited typing exercise, February 1964):** *I really get edgy when I am being idle. I have to have something I am working on and heading for, or finishing up, or planning to do (like now or in five minutes)...*

**Sandy Chapin:** Here's an example of Harry at home relaxing. He'd be listening to a basketball game and he'd be writing a lyric at the same time. This was not unusual. Sometimes he got together with his brothers — there were family things. Mostly what he did with the kids is take them to sports events. We also did some plays and some Broadway shows. Sometimes school events. Both Jono and Jason were varsity captains and he got to a lot of their games because he could still get to an evening concert a good part of the time.

Here's an example of Harry relaxing. Everything he did he had to conquer the universe. So he liked to take a Caribbean vacation. But every time had to be a different island. My feeling about this was, OK, the first day you're traveling; the second day you figure out where the heck am I? Which island is this? You kind of get a little oriented. The next day you're on vacation; and the next day we're leaving because they were always three or four day vacations.

The way Harry operated, he's working the whole time. He's working the phones at the airport until he jumps on the plane. He's working on the plane the whole time and then we'd get there — he called them writing vacations and they were three or four days — and he's on the phone when we get there and he's writing, and then he's working and writing, and then we go back to the airport. As soon as he gets off the plane, he's on the phone again and working on whatever is happening later that day; the next day. That was his idea of relaxation.

One time he came home and he said, 'I was reading this article ... about A-type personalities and it says [when] an A-type needs to take a vacation, that they need a minimum of 10 days to two weeks in order to really shut down and relax.' So he said, 'It's your responsibility that from now on when I take a vacation it's got to be 10 days or two weeks.' That was his announcement.

I always remember that one. That was one of the best — 'It's your responsibility to see that I take a vacation of at least 10 days.'

**Jaime Chapin Miller (Daughter):** Harry was a force of nature. We never knew what would happen next when he blew in the door. Would we be going bowling? On a boat ride? Planning our next family trip? Or something else?

**Elspeth Hart (Mother):** He was always sort of gulping something down to get to the next thing.

**Bill Ayres (Friend; Co-founder, WhyHunger):** We're sitting in his house. It's winter, there's snow on the ground. There's a call from one of the kids to pick him up. Harry gets up right away — doesn't have any shoes on — and runs through the snow barefoot and drives to pick the kid up. I said, 'What the hell's the matter with you? Why don't you wear shoes?' He said, 'Well, I put the heat on in the car.' I never would have thought to do that. I would have put shoes on first, but not him.

One of his great lines, which I use often, is 'Surprise me, I love surprises.'

**Jason Chapin:** We liked to go on family vacations and my mother always wanted to make them educational. We went to Greece and learned all about Greek history. We went to Egypt and visited the pyramids. And then he'd start incorporating some tours because my uncle was in the military. So he was performing on a lot of military bases in Europe. We would go do some sightseeing and some tour stuff in the day. Then he would do a concert at night. Then we'd go on to another country or another city and repeat the whole thing for about a week or 10 days.

I remember another European vacation where he invited a lot of his uncles and a lot of my uncles and aunts and their families, so there was something like 17 of us in two VW buses going from place to place. It was a little chaotic but very memorable. I think there was one trip in England with some other relatives and then there was another trip in Germany and maybe France.

**Sandy Chapin:** He was very much a Pied Piper. I think it's a trick for parenting — if you do something that you really enjoy doing, then the crossover to the kids is going to take hold. Harry always did that. You know, he used to always like doing something that he enjoyed and saying, 'Hey, this is going to be fun,' and getting them all in this. So he did homework; he did swimming lessons. He taught each one of them to swim out at Andover. And then a lot of just packing everybody into the car. A lot of sports with the guys later on.

**Jen Chapin (Daughter):** His hit song was "Cat's in the Cradle." He had his hypocrisy in his face every single day. He definitely made up for it in a lot of ways when he was home. I say that even though I didn't get to be a teenager because he died when I was 10, I got a preview of that experience of being completely horrified by your parents at a young age because he embarrassed me so terribly as an 8-year-old.

**Jaime Chapin Miller:** He had a great parenting style — 'We're going on an adventure. You're going to have a great time. And you're going to thank me for it!' This was often met with groans: 'Uh-oh, what next?'

**Jen Chapin:** We were always going somewhere. He would come home and then be instantly like, 'OK, where are we going? We're going bowling.' 'Daddy, I don't want to go bowling.' 'You want to go bowling; I heard you in your sleep last night saying, 'I want to go bowling! I want to go bowling!' C'mon, c'mon, let's go!' Always activities — keep it moving; keep it going; build a project; go to a restaurant.

The normal thing was like going on some crazy thing. I always say we're the only family that went to every museum in Hawaii.

**Patrick Leahy (Friend; U.S. senator):** A lot of times [when] Harry would be doing a concert or meeting in Washington; he'd stay at our home. Our youngest ... had an outsized Harry Chapin T-shirt. He actually wore that as his pajamas, like a nightshirt. He liked Harry so much — so much so that one night the phone rings and he answers. The voice goes, 'Mark Patrick Leahy?' He didn't recognize the voice. Harry goes, "The cat's in the cradle and the silver spoon." He goes, 'Harry! Harry! Where are you, Harry?' 'I'm in Australia, but I was talking with your father earlier today and he said you had been sick so I thought I would give you a call before my concert goes on.'

Can you imagine? The guy's about to go into a concert in another country. He heard that Mark wasn't feeling well — so he called him.

When (Harry) was killed, Mark took that T-shirt, rolled it up, and put it in the dresser. Never wore it again. It's still there. The kids were all brokenhearted.

* * *

# SEQUEL

**Fred Kewley (First manager):** Had I been there, I would have really fought against ("Sequel"). I mean that looked like a last gasp at riding some old wave.

**Howard Albert (Co-producer, *Sequel*):** We just went in there with the idea ... and just knocked it out. You can't read any more into it than what it was.

**Ken Kragen (Second manager):** Part of the problem was that I was in the midst of the heyday of Kenny Rogers. Then I signed Lionel Richie. So I had two of the biggest and hottest artists in the country who I was personally handling. It was when (Harry) wasn't getting the airplay or the sales that he had been. Although we mapped out some pretty good campaigns with the record company, I don't think we ever really achieved any huge breakthrough. I wasn't there during that period of time when things really broke big for him.

**Nancy Heller (Friend):** The albums never really were able to convey Harry the same way as interacting with him in person.

**Ron Albert (Co-producer, *Sequel*):** We did this album [*Sequel*] sort of as a tag-team event. We had to fly around and chase Harry.

We were recording in Canada. My favorite Harry story is we would go to the studio; usually start around 11 a.m. or 12 p.m.; work until 10 or 11 at night; and then go home; get up the next morning; and come back. We were working in the studio in Canada and I got up in the morning to take a shower — it must have been like 8 o'clock, 9 o'clock. When we got to the studio, I said, 'Ah, Harry, I saw you on TV this morning — you must have been up early.' Harry says to me, 'You saw me on TV — which channel?' I said, 'On Channel 7. Why?' He goes, 'Well, I did an interview before that on Channel 10.'

He had done two TV interviews ... before we had even woken up.

Harry was recording in Miami and would work until 10 o'clock at night; jump on the airplane; fly to New York so he could see his kids and take them to school; and fly back to Miami. Of course, this is before 9/11 restrictions.

He had his own tickets. If the airplane was full, he would

sit in the jump seat.

**Howard Albert:** He was always 110 percent on everything all the time.

**Ron Albert:** *Sequel* was certainly a great way of promoting Harry's talents and his process of making many, many albums, but there's a song on there called "Remember When the Music," which is really a song that Harry felt so strongly about. "Sequel" is great. People loved it. It got a lot of airplay. But "Remember When the Music" is one of my favorites.

If Harry could have had a hit off that album, I think he would have chosen that song because it was so near and dear to his heart.

Quite frankly, I don't think there's a more talented, more humble person that we've ever worked with. And we've worked with a lot of artists.

❊ ❊ ❊

**Sandy Chapin:** Harry was very frantic in 1980 because he was doing benefit concerts for congressmen who supported food and nutrition issues, whether they were Democrats or Republicans.

**David Miller (Friend):** Harry and Bill founded World Hunger Year in 1975. Then in 1980, Harry started Long Island Cares, sort of the extension to World Hunger Year. Harry said, 'Well, you know, how can you have hunger if you can't prevent it in your own backyard first?'

Harry wanted to matter and there's no doubt that he did,

for sure.

**Byron Dorgan (Friend; Former U.S. senator):** I was considering running for Congress and he said to me, 'If you do that, let me come out and raise some money for you. Let me help you raise the money. I'd love to see you elected. Congress would be better with you there.'

So he came to North Dakota and did a concert for me at the University of North Dakota. Twenty-four hundred people showed up to an auditorium that held 2,400 people. He flew in — wouldn't even allow me to pay for his plane ticket. He said, 'Just borrow a Martin guitar from the local music store; that's all I need.' He did a two-and-a-half hour concert to 2,400, raised a substantial amount of money for my campaign, and, in many ways, it was not political.

I was elected in the 1980 election.

**Big John Wallace:** I remember later on — maybe close to the end in '81 — when maybe we'd come back to a place and there were less people than there were the year before, that kind of thing. You could see it in his eyes. I remember a few times he had a little bit of a haunted look about him. But that was at the end.

**Jen Chapin:** He didn't care about sleep, and you really hear it. Like if you ever hear *The Bottom Line Encore Collection*, his voice is completely shot. He didn't have enough hours in the day.

**Allan Pepper (Co-owner, The Bottom Line):** (Harry) was normally very, very intense. He was a really intense guy and for this engagement [*The Bottom Line Encore Collection*], it seemed that he really wanted to do it. He was very relaxed. He was very accessible to the fans. It just seemed to be very important to him. Depending on when you met him and when you bumped into him, (Harry) could be charming; he could be funny; he could be short; he could be abrasive. He could be a mixture of different emotions, which is why that engagement, I thought, was so special because he really wanted to be there.

The people were with him from the jump. He walked out on the stage — you know, he had them. He'd be singing and you'd see them all vocalizing. You'd see people in their chairs singing along with him. Whether it was "Taxi" or whether it was "Bananas," they'd sing out and sing along with him. So listen, you're celebrating your 2,000th performance, you have an adoring audience — an audience you can't do any wrong with — who wouldn't be happy, you know? It was a great, festive three days.

**Shelly Schultz:** Normally he wouldn't play a club, but he was playing a club because he released a new record and he was doing the record. And, as always, Harry's shows were really long. He loved to do long shows and he loved to talk. I was sitting with a colleague of mine, one of the guys who worked for me, and he said, 'You know, Harry's shows are great. The first 45 minutes are great.' And I said, 'And the next four 45 minutes' will kill you.' We always used to laugh about it.

**Bill Ayres:** I was involved in trying to help Harry kind of balance his life out. As you know, I was a Roman Catholic priest at the time. So I had the experience of counseling. Harry — who was an admitted agnostic; came from an agnostic family — thought it was really cool he was operating with the rock and roll priest. We were kind of an interesting pair.

The last big thing that he did in his life musically was something called *Cotton Patch Gospel*. He talked to me a lot about that and I helped him with it. It was based on the Gospels.

Harry said to me, 'People ask me why I'm doing this. Am I doing it because I'm a believer?' He said, 'What I tell them is, 'I believe in the believers.' I have been so taken by people with religious beliefs who are working hard to fight hunger and poverty. They are the people doing it.'

He never became a member of a church or anything, but he certainly was more open to ... the spiritual part of reality. We spent a lot of time talking about that over the years.

**Tom Chapin (Brother):** (*Cotton Patch Gospel*) ran for several months in New York City at Lamb's Theatre. Now it's on what we like to call the "Eternity Tour." Various places around the country put it on all the time. It's a wonderful show. It really is.

**Sandy Chapin:** His last album was going to be a film score and he was going to finally make the feature films that he always wanted to make. He always kind of pictured himself as a Hollywood director and participated in one film called *Mother and Daughter: The Loving War*. He somehow had this idea in the back of his head that he was going to be a Hollywood film writer/director.

**Charles Sanders (Friend; Producer, *1987 Carnegie Hall Tribute to Harry Chapin*):** Harry was certainly a fatalist. I think anybody who flew in small planes as much as he did expects eventually to have a problem with that, and I think that he knew that.

He also made reference in several songs — one of them being a very long piece on *Dance Band on the Titanic* called "There Only Was One Choice" where he talked about his 34th birthday and getting up in the morning and thinking that he's not Mozart, he's not Keats, and what a bummer that was for him that he had outlived those two.

I think in that reference, there was an expectation that he expected great things of himself and he expected to burn out going for it.

**Nancy Heller:** He was big. He lived big. He died big.

**Howard Fields:** We played with him right until the end. We were about to start a huge summer tour at the usual places we played at and we were looking forward to it. We had about a month off and then we were supposed to do the July 16th show out in Eisenhower Park in Long Island. That was the night of his fatal accident. But following that it would have been a whole summer tour.

❈ ❈ ❈

**Jason Chapin:** It may have been our second trip to Hawaii. I remember we went to Oahu and we were up in Turtle Bay. Then we were at a hotel. There was a little bit of surfing. We went golfing one day and we had a lot of nice meals. I remember one time we went out to dinner and Alan Alda was there so my father went over and said hello to him. I remember that it was very relaxing.

**Jono Chapin:** We went to a Polynesian Cultural Center, which was pretty fascinating. Everything from eating poi and understanding the different islands and the different cultural traditions that various islands had was pretty cool.

We went surfing and I can remember Harry's stance up on a surfboard was instead of sideways where you think of skateboarding or snowboarding or so on; as I recall it, he was up on the board facing directly forward and that's how he was sort of balancing on the board. If I recall, it worked.

I'm sure everybody remembers this because we were all out there and not too happy about it after a while. Harry was probably one of those people that had a little bit more experience than the rest of us and I was probably in a little bit of a macho phase, but there was a deep sea fishing boat excursion that was planned, I think, sort of towards the end of the trip. I think it was suggested you could take maybe Dramamine, but I seem to remember choosing not to take the Dramamine and I paid for it, as I believe other people did.

We got there — I don't think we were all that far offshore, but the swells were so big that when the boat was at the bottom of the swell you could not see land or the horizon line.... Harry was strapped in and taking the Dramamine and was about as happy as a clam, and hooked in a marlin. I don't know how long the fight was, but that sustained me. I mean you're hurting when some of that motion sickness is really hitting hard, but he pulled that marlin in. We got to shore and it was a pretty good-sized marlin, to my recollection. The spear of that; God, it must have been three- or four-feet long.

**Josh Chapin:** I remember a lot about that trip. I remember the deep sea fishing. I was a little seasick. I remember my mom taught me to look out on the horizon to make me feel better. I remember golfing and somehow parring on a Par 3. I remember the golf pro my dad was playing with saying that I had such a beautiful, natural swing and how I could be a pro golfer.

We were at the driving range — and this is one of those stories that no one can confirm but it's pretty funny — I think my brother Jason shanked one — went off the tip of the driver or something — and bounced through some trees onto some pavement and through a car window like this big, and hit some woman in the head. Somehow we had to go over there and my dad had to apologize. It was absolutely ridiculous. It was completely a *Caddyshack* moment.

He'd usually combine (a vacation) with a tour, so I guess this was one of the few times when he wasn't singing or doing a performance there. But yeah, it was a great trip.

**Sandy Chapin:** He was home one night and the next day he was on the way to the city to meetings. We came home the day before he died.

I think he pretty much was calmed down. The original plan was that we were all going to go to Australia because he was going to have a tour. For some reason, the tour fell through. I think enough of it didn't go into place to make it financially viable. So he had the time set aside. Then he said to the kids, 'OK, we have 10 days' — or whatever it was — 'Where do you want to go?' I don't know what the different suggestions were, but anyway it ended up [being] Hawaii.

I would say that it was a complete vacation because he didn't have any concerts. He didn't have anything to do but sports, recreation, and toying around.

# CHAPTER 9

## *EMPTY*

**Tom Chapin (Brother):** The biggest thing for me was when Harry died, the universe cracked a little bit for us.

I was the one that got the phone call. I was not surprised, but I was shocked.

**Rex Fowler (Musician, Aztec Two-Step):** I don't remember exactly when we rode in the car with him, but ... no one who knew Harry personally who had ever driven with Harry was shocked or surprised that he got into this terrible car accident. He might have been the world's worst driver because he was the original multitasker. He literally would sit there and type on his typewriter, and drive the car, and carry on conversations — weaving in and out of traffic — scaring the living bejesus out of everyone in the car.

**Sandy Chapin (Wife):** What I do remember is that Jason had a job with a lumber company in town. He came in to our bedroom and he said, 'Which car do you want me to take?' I said right away the van, because Harry didn't have a reputation for being the best kind of driver. The other car was my daughter Jaime's VW Rabbit, I guess it was. He said, 'No, no, no, I want to take the Rabbit because I want to listen to music,' because I guess she had a pretty good tape system. So he lost and Jason went to work in the van. Harry took off in the Rabbit, which, to the best of our knowledge, broke down even though it had just come out of the shop.

I had used the car to go to a Long Island Cares meeting before we went to Hawaii. I had noticed that it decelerated while I was driving. So I made a point of staying way over in the right-hand lane. I did get to my meeting. I did get home and then it hadn't happened again. I remember that I had mentioned that when the car went in.

**Jason Chapin (Son):** I did have a feeling that something strange was going on because it was just very quiet. I don't know who was home at the time, but I remember ... there was a phone call, and then there were a couple of other phone calls. Then my father's assistant, Don Ruthig, came over some time around lunchtime and sat down in the upstairs TV room with ... my brother Jono and myself, and said that he had to tell us some news.

He told us that my father was in the accident and they took him to the hospital. I think Don told us that they tried to save him but that he had died. From that point on, it seemed like it was very crazy because there were lots of phone calls and lots of people coming by and there was, you know, stuff on TV and radio, and friends coming over. There was very little time to really absorb that he had died.

I remember I went for a walk down to the beach and I was just by myself for about three hours trying to figure out how this was all going to change our lives with him gone, and the whole shock of it all.

I think just like any other family that deals with a sudden death, there was shock. We were all trying to understand that this was really happening. Then at the same time what made it a little different for us was that because he was famous, a lot of other people found out as soon as we did. So there were people coming by and trying to offer their support. So we weren't really together as a family and alone; we were together as a family with a lot of other people. We were kind of all aware that we were together but not really able to talk to each other and to see how we were doing. It was really, I think, a few days until we were really able to see how we were all doing.

**Don Ruthig (Personal assistant):** He died on my birthday. He was supposed to be at my house for a birthday party for a big barbecue. Sandy was over there with the kids. We were all setting up for the barbecue and Harry was missing. Sandy went home for some reason to pick up something and then I got the news that Harry had been killed. I had to go over and tell Sandy, and all that. That was ... a horrendous day.

I think our booking agent at that point was ICM. (Harry) was on his way into the city to have a meeting with his booking agent and he didn't show up.

**Shelly Schultz (Booking agent):** He was coming to have lunch and I called [Harry's brother] Jeb [Hart]. I said, 'Jeb, where is he?' He was like an hour late. He said, 'I thought you heard,' or something. Anyhow that's how we found out. That was terrible.

**Josh Chapin (Son):** It was Don Ruthig's birthday. Harry

had a few morning meetings and he had a concert that night, but then he was supposed to show up at this place in the next town over. He never showed up and people were getting more and more nervous. Then we went back to my house and I think a few people started to find out. I think after they found out, somebody was trying to get me out of the house — I guess they wanted to get a game plan or something for the kids, I'm not quite sure — but someone tried to get me out of the house.

We were going to do a Burger King run. So we went to Burger King and then ... we stopped at 7-Eleven and they played "Cat's in the Cradle." Just [from] the whole aura about the whole day, I knew that he was dead. I actually knew.

I prepared myself somehow at that moment — just the whole combination of events of the day because he was supposed to show up some time around noon and it was like 4 p.m.

**Don Ruthig:** Jeb and his partner, Bob Hinkle, finally found out what happened. I think they finally got in touch with the police and found out that he had been in the accident on the Expressway. So Jebbie called me and confirmed what we kind of already ... were fearing, that something serious had happened.

I grabbed Josh, who was swimming in the pool at my house, and I took him home. He went upstairs and then I told Sandy what was going on. Sandy just kind of shut down initially. I think she was so shocked. I don't think she sat down with Josh and Jenny and told them until probably several hours later. His daughter Jaime was still in Hawaii. They got in touch with Jaime and she got on a flight back from Hawaii. I don't think I went home. I got to their house and after I told Sandy, I didn't go home for several days because the whole process had started of people coming to the house.

I don't know whether the band was there yet or not, but yeah, they were all coming to my place. We were going to have a barbecue and then we were going to Eisenhower Pavilion at Salisbury Park. It was a group show, so it wasn't a benefit, I don't think, that night.

**Howard Fields (Drummer):** That show was set up for Eisenhower Park — free concert — out in Long Island. So we set up early. Harry's right-hand man was a fella named Don Ruthig, who had been working for him for a few years, and set up his daily schedule. So I was at his house ... and all I can tell you is my experience was that I was hanging out and walking into the house and Don was sitting there in his living room looking a little odd. I didn't think much of it.... But the phone rang and he lunged for it. I don't remember the words he was saying, but he hung up the phone and he broke down in tears and says, 'It was him. He's dead.' He had evidently gotten a phone call some time earlier, which put him in that odd mood. He was told that there was an accident and it was believed that Harry Chapin was involved in it. It was very serious. So they called Don and he was just waiting for confirmation. That was the phone call he got while I was in the room, which caused him to fall to tears.

I know Doug Walker was there. John Wallace arrived a little bit later and found out about it. Then I guess from there we went back to the venue where the crowd had already started gathering for the concert. I remember there was a New York promoter named Howard Stein

— he was involved in putting this pre-show together — and he made the announcement to the crowd that Harry Chapin was involved in a fatal car accident. It was a very odd thing. I mean our sound company was there and I said to myself, 'Geez, I guess I'd better take my drums home with me.' It was a very odd little moment because otherwise all our equipment would go with them and for the whole summer we'd be doing shows with them hauling our equipment around. I just remember that.

From there, I remember my mom and dad were at that show and we were heading to Harry's house. I was in my car and I saw them. They were right on the road that I was driving on and they said, 'What's going on, where are you going?' I said, 'I got to go to Harry's. I'm going to Harry's house.' I said, 'I have to follow these cars or otherwise I don't know where I'm going.' I had to like really kind of drive away from there.

We went to his house and stayed there and the house really started filling up with people. I remember Harry, Tom, and Steve's dad Jim was there — Jim Chapin — and I remember him breaking down at one point in the evening. I remember Garry Trudeau was there — the *Doonesbury* guy. He was there. They were friends. It was quite a full house.

**From "Singer-Activist Harry Chapin Killed by Fiery Collision on LIE,"** *Newsday* **– July 17, 1981:** *Harry Chapin, singer-songwriter and a keystone in the Long Island cultural arts scene, died yesterday, the victim of a fiery crash of his car and a tractor-trailer on the Long Island Expressway.*

*The 38-year-old Chapin of Huntington Bay, who suffered a massive internal hemorrhage from a lacerated aorta, was pronounced dead at Nassau County Medical Center at 1:07 p.m.*

*Death came in a swerve, a crash, an explosion, and a burst of flames that turned a pleasant summer's day into a chaotic horror. Chapin was killed at 12:29 p.m. while driving westbound on the Long Island Expressway near Exit 40 in Jericho. Swerving from the left lane to the center lane, Chapin was struck from the rear by a truck unable to brake in time. The car burst into flames and was pushed 300 feet to the right side of the expressway. Several rescuers dragged Chapin from the burning wreckage after the driver whose truck collided with Chapin's Volkswagen used a pocket knife to cut away the seat belt that held Chapin in his seat.*

**Sandy Chapin:** I had a premonition there was something somebody was not telling me and there was something wrong. I mean if I look back, it's very odd that I was in this cocoon. I was definitely definitively in a cocoon. I didn't turn on the radio or anything like that.... I think at a certain point there probably was something on the news, but I wasn't tuning into anything. So that's as much as I remember about it. His fans came out because they were waiting at Eisenhower Park. It was all pretty crazy for a few days.

**Josh Chapin:** I mean it's crazy when somebody dies when you're eight. It's like he's the same size as me almost exactly. When you're locked in as an 8-year-old, I just think of him as this giant, you know. When that happened — yeah I just cried. It was a big moment for me because I cried my eyes out for probably less than five minutes. That was the grieving I did. After that, I remember spending a lot of time trying to make people like laugh or feel good. So it was a little weird.

I felt a lot of guilt afterwards because I'd go to school and my friends would be like, 'I cried for three days after your dad died,' and I'm like, 'Shit, I only cried for five minutes.' Everybody grieves differently, obviously.

I also realized how I felt about religion and God and having the dual message of the whole thing—'Your dad is the most amazing man that ever was.' Then you had religious people coming up to you saying, 'Everything happens for a reason.' I remember as an 8-year-old, trying to reconcile those two points and be like, 'Well, what was the reason then?' So I definitely had thought that all day and I just didn't want to have anybody or I didn't want anybody else talking about God. I was definitely off of God for at least that day and the immediate future.

I think there were questions I would have asked of him on the way I grew up. Obviously, there is the very daunting thought process of this is a man who, more than anybody I've ever known, did more in a 10-year period in terms of being effective or being productive or trying, you know — a just nonstop whirlwind of effort than anybody out there. So how do I admire that? I think about it as a brilliant way to live, but also not making myself crazy trying to carve out my own existence.

**Don Ruthig:** Harry loved all the kids, but Josh particularly was the light of his life. Josh looked like Harry. He had Harry's chin. Harry wrote a song called "Dancin' Boy" because Josh used to come up on the stage and ... do this sort of rocking back and forth, dancing to Harry's music.

**Bill Ayres (Friend; Co-founder, WhyHunger):** I was in

Massachusetts, up around Fall River. It was the summertime in July and my wife asked me to go up with our little baby to visit her family. They hadn't seen the baby.

We drove up there and we were staying at one of her cousins' house. We had gone to the beach that day and for some reason, I just had this very kind of down feeling. I'm not that kind of person. My wife said, 'What's the matter with you?' I said, 'I don't know. Just ... I don't know.'

We're getting ready for dinner and her cousin's husband came up and said, 'I don't know how to tell you this,' he said, 'But I just was looking on the television and your friend Harry Chapin died in an automobile accident.' I went down and, sure enough, it was true. I said to my wife, 'We have to go.' We put the baby in the car and I called Sandy and said, 'I'll be over.' I drove home. I don't know how I did it with the tears and everything but I did. It was a very traumatic time, but people came through and helped us out.

**Dave Marsh (Friend; Music critic):** One day I walked into Crazy Eddie's down the street from my apartment and somebody made a very bad joke about Harry dying in a car crash. I said, 'That's not funny.' He said he wasn't joking about that part. I burst into tears and ran home. Literally ran home. That's the frame of the story.

It was just a horrible thing to happen. This was not a person I wanted to depart this earth early.

**Thomas Downey (Friend; Former U.S. representative):** I remember thinking that God must be angry with us for some reason to take away Harry Chapin.

**Stanley Snadowsky (Co-owner, The Bottom Line):** I'll

never forget. I'll never forget. I was walking to the club and I heard a radio that said Harry Chapin was killed on the Long Island Expressway. The world was really cheated by his early death because he probably had so much more to give in terms of his entertainment.

**Gordon Lightfoot (Musician):** I was in the bush that summer for a month. When I got out of the bush I heard about it by staff. When I'm in the bush, I'm incommunicado.

It was one of the first things I heard. The article was sitting on my desk.... I was saddened and I felt badly, and I thought, 'What an awful way to have to go.' That was really the first thing that hit my mind. I felt very sorry.

**Patrick Leahy (Friend; U.S. senator):** This was back before everybody had cell phones and iPhones and so on. [I'm] sitting on the [Senate] Floor and one of the young people working in the cloakroom came out and tapped me on the shoulder. She said, 'Senator, we have something to show you. I think you'd better come in the cloakroom. We don't want to show you out here.'

We actually had wire service, and they pulled the thing off the wire and they handed it to me. I read very fast. I read it, and read it, and read it. I just — I'm getting choked up now — I sat there and I just cried. We had phones in there. I called Marcelle and she was sobbing. I just went home as quickly as I could.

I'm looking at a picture of him here where I am right now. I mean this hit me harder than I ever thought something could.

**Ken Kragen (Second manager):** Harry was an important person in my life. I mean his loss meant a lot to me. It really shook me, although I will tell you when I heard of Harry's death, I was on the road with Kenny Rogers in Ames, Iowa. I got on the phone immediately and by the time I hung up a few hours later, I had raised $200,000 to continue the charity work he was doing. I called people who admired Harry and got them to pledge contributions; told them that Harry had been killed and then traded immediately on that shock and grief to get them to help continue Harry's work. I recognized that there was going to be a small window of opportunity there to do that and that there was a huge need. I think also I just sort of was in a situation where it felt like, 'I've got to do something, I can't just sit here.' So I just spent afternoon in Ames, Iowa making that kind of thing happen.

Either Jeb or Bob called me and said Harry was killed on the Long Island Expressway. At that point things were a little vague as to what had happened.

We knew later that he was driving without a license.

**From "Singer-Activist Harry Chapin Killed by Fiery Collision on LIE,"** *Newsday* – **July 17, 1981:** *Chapin had no identification on his body at the time of the accident. State Department of Motor Vehicle records show Chapin's license was revoked on March 1. The revocation was only the latest infraction in Chapin's erratic driving record, according to the state records.*

*His license was revoked for a year on Nov. 5, 1976, after which he was put on probation. His license was suspended four times between July 5, 1975 and July 11, 1980. From*

*1973, he was convicted at least 15 times for speeding, improper passing, failure to signal, operating without a license, operating a vehicle with a suspended license, and driving an unregistered motor vehicle. The traffic violations occurred in New York, Queens, Nassau, Suffolk, and Warren Counties.*

**Tom Chapin:** I was the one who got the news. I lived ... right by the Brooklyn Bridge in an apartment right underneath Hart and Hinkle, who were managing Harry. They were in the top floor, fifth floor. I was on the fourth floor. Hart and Hinkle were waiting for Harry to have a meeting with his booking agent in Manhattan. I was down there alone and there was a brand new secretary who was there alone. I get a knock of the door and she said, 'Tom, would you come up here please because it's about Harry.' So I went upstairs, got on the phone. I said, 'Hello?' And this cop says, 'Who's this?' I said, 'Tom Chapin, who are you?' I said, 'What's the matter?' We talked a minute and they were trying to identify the body.

I'll tell you what identified it. It was a watch that Michael Moore gave Harry for doing a benefit to start his Flint, Michigan newspaper. Harry did a bunch of benefits for him and he gave him a watch. He didn't have his wallet on him.

The car was Jaime's car. It was a VW Rabbit. But there was a watch from the *Flint Voice,* and I said it was Harry. The guy said, 'Well, you need to come out and identify the body.' I said, 'OK.' So then I got off the phone and I called Jeb. The secretary said, 'Jebbie's been calling, trying to have me track Harry down.' So I called Jeb — they were at this booking agent's office in Manhattan — and Jeb goes, 'That's not his car!' I said, 'No, it's Jaime's car.' So we started calling around and just telling people stuff. I was very centered; as I say, I was shocked but not surprised. I called my wife and she was out with the two little girls. Lily was two weeks old — my youngest daughter — and she was out visiting a friend with Abigail, who was two at that point.

Then there's various phone calls back and forth. Then Jeb and Steve call. Then I call out to Jersey because it's July, you know, and my brother James is there.... Then finally James calls back and I talk to him about it.

My mother was working still out at Garland Publishing and it's now about 4 o'clock, so she's getting home really quickly. I talked to Steve and Jeb and they said, 'We'll go identify the body; you go tell Mom.' I said, 'The guy wants you to go right away.' Steve says, 'There's no hurry. Harry's going nowhere. We'll go out there when we get there.' Steve and Jeb went out there to identify the body. So I tell ... the secretary. I go down the house, put a coat on and grab some stuff, and I run up to my mother's apartment and I go inside. I get there just as she's arriving — 'Oh, isn't this nice to see you.' I said, 'Ma, I got some bad news.' She goes, 'The baby?' 'Nope, she's fine. It's Harry,' and then she goes 'Ugh!' and sits.

**Elspeth Hart (Mother):** Tom came to tell me. I was coming back from work. I got off at the Hotel St. George and Tom was there. He says, 'Something awful has happened.' We walked to the house, we went in, and I think that then he said, 'It's Harry.'

I turned on the TV for some reason and there on the TV it said that Harry Chapin had been killed. I just couldn't understand it. Why? How? It doesn't make any sense.

**Tom Chapin:** We decided we're all going to end up in New Jersey because that's where everybody is in the summertime.... We're driving out and there's this incredible sunset; just these gigantic pink clouds. It was unbelievable. We're driving into the sunset, driving in the west, and we get there. I come up to the house and I've been really sober the whole way through. Get to the house, walk up into the house, and the whole family is there. I said, 'Wow I thought James was here alone.'

I lost it.

**Jim Chapin (Nephew):** I was down at the beach with my dad and my younger brother. I was, I guess, almost 10 and my brother was seven and ... my great-uncle came down and whispered in my dad's ear something or other. Then my dad shouted, 'Shit, Harry's dead!' [He] then walked away and started walking up the road. We followed and I remember my brother asking me, 'Could it be another Harry?' They said, 'No, no, it's definitely your uncle.'

It was the first time I ever saw my dad cry, I remember.

**From "Singer-Activist Harry Chapin Killed by Fiery Collision on LIE,"** *Newsday* **– July 17, 1981:** *Six hours later, thousands of fans pouring into Eisenhower Park's Lakeside Theater expecting to hear Chapin in concert wept upon hearing the announcement: 'The concert has been canceled because of the tragic death of Harry Chapin.'*

**Nancy Heller (Friend):** There was a song I had written that we worked on together that weekend that (Harry) wanted to give to Pete Seeger. The tape of the song was in my bag to give to him the day he died.

**Big John Wallace (Bassist):** We wound up going back to Eisenhower Park. I think we just kind of wandered up on stage and then somebody made the announcement, or maybe they had known already, I'm not sure. The people were just standing there milling around too. I don't think we played or unpacked or anything, but the people kind of joined hands in this big circle and walked around this big circle. That's all that I remember of that day.

**From "A Stunned Audience At the Park,"** *Newsday* **– July 17, 1981:** *At 8:25 p.m., after the stage crew had gone home, several thousand of the 25,000 fans who had been expected to attend the concert huddled quietly in small groups. A crowd gathered in a circle around Nancy Heller, 17, of East Northport, as she played one of Chapin's songs, "All My Life's a Circle" [sic], on her guitar. They sang enthusiastically and passed a lighted candle around the circle.*

*'He inspired me to write my first song,' Ms. Heller said. 'I came up to him at a concert and said, 'Will you be my friend?' He said. 'Forever friends.' My God, how he touched me.'*

**Nancy Heller:** I went down to the backstage area to see who was there, to see if anybody I knew was there. The family was not there. The band members, the manager was there. Then I came back out and the people next to me; among the things they had in their cooler was some beer. I asked them for a beer and drank a couple of them. With a little liquid courage there was another guy on the other side who had an Ovation guitar and he was playing, "Bye, bye Miss American Pie." I walked up to him emboldened by the beer; grabbed the guitar out of his hands; said, 'You're playing the wrong songs;' and started playing Harry's music.

The next thing I know, people are in a circle around me singing. It was a pretty surreal experience, you know. We kind of had our own little memorial. A few hundred people there singing "All my life's a circle," and "Cat's in the Cradle," and other things, just trying to cope with a very, very sad situation.

I had just turned 17.

**Marie "Peachie" Marsden (Friend):** I remember Steve hugging us and saying, 'You have to help us do this. We don't know how to do this.'

We're Irish Catholics and what we do is we mourn privately. But usually we have a party to celebrate a person's life. So that's what we would do about Harry. We would celebrate his life because his life was beautiful.

❈ ❈ ❈

**Don Ruthig:** The funeral director was a friend. He had kids Josh and Jenny's age and they were friends. Chris [Jacobsen] was great in helping us get things together.

I said something to Sandy about, 'What's he going to be dressed in? Do you have a suit?' And she said, 'Oh no, we're not putting him in a suit. He never wore a suit in his life; he's not going to wear one for his funeral.' So he was dressed in just a blue Oxford shirt open at the neck. Loafers. I don't think they were jeans; I think they were something like khakis. I just remember the blue Oxford shirt.

**Chris Jacobsen (Funeral director, A.L. Jacobsen Funeral Home):** Harry was a great guy, a great father, a real person.

Nice to be around. No airs. A genuine all-around nice guy. If you didn't know who he was, he wouldn't be anything at all. He was just a down-to-earth, real-life guy who loved his family and his kids and was there for games and everything. It's not like what you're seeing in the papers with stars having problems.... If you could have known him and met him you would have liked him. The whole thing was a major tragedy for the whole community.

**Shelly Schultz:** I remember tons of people and everybody was in shock because here was a guy who gave so much who left too early. The thing that occurred to me was that I don't think his family got the best of him. Not because he didn't want to; he had priorities. I never spoke to Sandy about that ever, ever because that's very personal. But my hunch is his family never got the best of him.

**Tom Chapin:** (Sandy) had the body lay out in state and, of course, it wasn't him except his hair. But it took away the shock of the accident, you know what I mean. You see something there that's in front of you so it's not him in terrible agony.

I walked up, and I just looked at him, and I touched his hair. I said, 'What was it, Harry? What was the fucking hurry?'

**Jason Chapin:** My mother — she's unbelievable; an incredible mother. She's very motherly, very protective of her children and always trying to figure out how they're doing. I think that she was conscious of what we were going through but, at the same time, I think she was trying to take care of us. At the same time, everyone was trying to see how she was doing and to see what she needed.

I don't think she really was able to spend a lot of time trying to think about what she felt. I think that must have been an extremely difficult time for her trying to deal with all of the things that she didn't expect she'd have to deal with.

Soon after she had to deal with the funeral and the service and the viewing. When I think someone's in that situation, I think they are just trying to get through. I don't think they are really able to step back and say, 'What's going on?' I think they are just going through one thing to another, and then they hope that after the funeral and after the service that they can then try and deal with everything they have to be able to deal with.

**Josh Chapin:** I mean they do amazing work, those people. He wasn't Sonny Corleone. I just remember his face anyway. That face meant vitality to me. I kissed him and seeing the cold, waxy lips ... it was really fucked up.

**Marie "Peachie" Marsden:** I was surprised that he looked so peaceful.... To see him peaceful made me feel so much better.

**Jason Chapin:** We had a private viewing, so I was very grateful that I was able to say goodbye to him. The casket was open.

**Robert Mrazek (Friend; Former U.S. representative):** It was an open casket and he looked like he was sleeping. It was a joke almost — like he was going to wake up and say, 'OK, the joke's on you!' But he looked absolutely untouched; unmarked; perfect.

**Don Ruthig:** There was the question of whether he'd be buried or cremated. If I recall correctly, he wanted to be cremated. But Sandy felt badly about that. She said he was so scattered in his life, he should be in one place in his death. So they buried him in a casket.

There was a huge rock out at the farm in Andover, New Jersey that Harry and the (boys) used to play on as kids. That became his headstone.

* * *

**Tom Chapin:** A week later we did the big memorial event at Grace Church. Some amazing people came and talked about Harry's legacy [and] what he meant to them, from Ralph Nader to Patrick Leahy, just down the line. Pete Seeger, you know — all these people. But the thing that really clarified everything for me was when my brother

## "HELLO, HONEY, IT'S ME"

James — who is now gone as well — got up and said, 'We can't fill Harry's shoes. We can't be Harry and even if we could, we wouldn't want to be. We can't fill his shoes but what we can do is fill our own shoes a little fuller.' That ... was really clarifying for me.

**From James Chapin's eulogy for Harry Chapin:** *I believe that my brother was a great man. But, unlike most other great men, his greatness did not come from diminishing those around him. He made himself great, in part, by finding the best in those around him. He made you feel important.*

*There's been a lot of talk about, 'How can we fill Harry's shoes?' The answer to that is that the challenge of Harry's life was NOT one of 'following in his footsteps' or 'filling his shoes.' The challenge is in filling our OWN shoes.*

*We carry on Harry's work not just because we loved and admired him. We do so because it is the proper work of us all.*

**Josh Chapin:** I was always kind of a ham. I remembered it being the first real memory of me being nervous and not wanting to get up and sing "Circle." He always could never stop me. I always was like, 'Oh yeah, definitely. I'll get up on stage.' Uncle Tom kind of gave me the option, I think, to do it or not, but I saw him start to cry. I got up from my seat and went to sing with him. That was the only personal memory I remember.

**Ken Kragen:** I was one of the memorial speakers. I had to do the eulogy for him at the memorial service. I remember having it pretty well together until I looked down and there were all the kids sitting right in front of me and they were crying. As I recall, I broke up at that point pretty badly.

**Patrick Leahy:** They asked me if I'd give one of the eulogies at his funeral in New York. Of course, I said I would. I was honored to do it, but it was one of the most difficult speeches I've ever made. I just wanted to talk about him. There were a lot of tears in that church that night.

**Big John Wallace:** I remember a little bit about the memorial in Grace Church but it was kind of a blur. I mean the shock came in and it set there, but it even took a long time for the shock to completely set in and for everybody to deal with it. So I don't have a lot of other memories at the time right after except coming home and seeing a higher counting on the old-fashioned message machine than I'd ever seen before. I remember that — 'Wow.' That was kind of nice, thinking about all those people that heard what happened and tried to reach out.

**Sandy Chapin:** I guess it was kind of a blur. I think it was certainly wonderful, but if I have any recollection, I think I just kept looking at my children's faces to see how they were doing. I remember certain things, but I was just very conscious of the children and how they were doing.

**Thomas Downey:** I remember everyone was sad, but I don't remember it being maudlin. When I said I met Harry Chapin through Allard Lowenstein — who said, '(Harry will) play for anybody' — that brought the house down. I didn't mean it as a joke but people wanted to laugh. There was enough crying. They wanted some relief.

**Marie "Peachie" Marsden:** Steve's coming back from Long Island at Sandy's house. We're heading to his house and what happened was he stopped. We're in the car behind him and we're saying, 'Oh what's he stopping for.' It was the crash site. He just had to have a moment there.

He pulled over — that's where the crash site was — and you could see where they had tried to work on Harry and like different things thrown on the ground. The car was gone, but the wreck was still there. Steve picked up what was the antenna and, for some reason, he thought it important because Harry was all about music and this is what we had left of him — just an antenna.

My sister Mary is the one that took it. She said, 'What are you going to do with that?' He said, 'I have no idea; I just picked it up.' She brought it to a friend of hers and this is what he did. He made a musical note out of it and we put a picture of Harry and [my husband] Zeke in it.

**Elspeth Hart:** I always wondered where he'd be if he hadn't died because I felt he was still at a crossroads with time.

**Dave Marsh:** Of all the people who passed on in music that I knew — Lester Bangs, Keith Moon, Fred Smith, Rob Tyner, Ron Asheton, Ruth Brown — I probably, on a consistent basis, think about Harry and miss him more than any of them. It's shocking to say that — even to me — but I think it's true because he left a mammoth legacy.

# CHAPTER 10

Harry Chapin
1942 – 1981

"Oh if a man tried
To take his time on earth
And prove before he died
What one man's life could be worth
I wonder what would happen
to this world."

## *YOU ARE THE ONLY SONG*

**Diana Chapin (Sister-in-law):** We made a will after our kids were born. Jim said later he was always happy he persuaded Harry to make out a will because he hadn't made out a will, and that if he hadn't done that before he died, his estate would have been a real problem for his kids.

**Anthony Curto (Attorney):** Harry died literally without

any money except for an insurance policy that was made to World Hunger Year, the charitable organization. So for all intents and purposes, the family was not destitute but without any funds. The only money that they really had was wrapped up in the lawsuit for the wrongful death case.

**Sandy Chapin (Wife):** I was definitely a different person. I'm pretty much a homebody and I remember that I would find something to do, some place to go like every evening. I mean eventually I got really depressed and I didn't want to move and I didn't want to leave the house, but initially it was kind of like being very manic.

**Anthony Curto:** When he died, Sandy, being socially conscious, wanted to make a statement similar to Ralph Nader's statement — that the Volkswagen that (Harry) was driving in wasn't properly seat-belted and didn't have a proper safety mechanism seat belt.

We started to work with safety groups in an attempt to bring action against Volkswagen, and also Supermarkets General who owned the truck that rear-ended him on the Long Island Expressway. He was hit from behind because his car was malfunctioning — nothing to do with the seat belts — and in the process of being hit from behind, the seat went backwards. Because there wasn't a lap belt in this Volkswagen, just an across the chest belt, he ramped up out of the cocoon of his seat, snapped his back and neck, causing a tear in his aorta. He was dead in about 15 seconds, 20 seconds.

The driver of the truck, in an attempt to save him, ran over to the car, which was burning, and got Harry out. As in an automobile accident case, you have a right to sue the driver and you have a right to sue the owner of the vehicle. The driver was never sued by the estate because of his heroic acts.

**Sandy Chapin:** I did not want to do it at all. There were a couple of people who had become very involved with our lives largely because of the boards that we were working with, mainly because of the Huntington Arts Council, which was very important to me. One of them was Tony Curto who put together the lawsuit. He came to me, and he was also talking to Harry's lawyer, Monte Morris. There were things happening that I didn't know about where the car was and who picked it up and what happened to it. Nobody spoke to me that things moved ahead — it was this lawyer, talking to this lawyer, talking to that lawyer, and certain things were being put in place. Then when they talked to me I said, 'No.' I did not want to get involved in a lawsuit.

What happened was Ralph Nader — he and Harry were very close — called me at something like 2 o'clock in the morning. It was very, very odd. He said it was very important; he had to talk to me. He said that I must get involved with this lawsuit against Volkswagen because he said he had for years brought up problems with the company, and then he said he would go and have meetings with them — with management — and he said they were very cavalier. They would say, 'Sue us. Go ahead sue.' And maybe he had or something. But anyway he was telling me this tale of woe and he said this is an opportunity to have the publicity. This is when he was advocating for seat belts. We forget that there were times like that that where there were no seat belts back then. I don't remember exactly what Volkswagen was doing. Then he said that he wanted to recommend the best product liability lawyer in the country, which he did.

Tony Curto talked to me and he said, 'I want to put together a team,' and then he talked to me about these three lawyers who would be involved.... Then I finally said yes, but all the money would go to the [Harry Chapin] Foundation. This was all set up. It was in a contract and I signed the contract.

Then the years went by and then on and on and on nothing happened. What eventually happened, as far as I understand, is that Volkswagen was apparently so good and hired such a good law firm that the information that I got was that my lawyers ended up feeling that they were going to lose the case. That was very disappointing. So now it was against Supermarkets General. One of the things that I said was it seemed OK to sue a huge corporation but ... that the driver must not be included. I would not sue an individual. Now I think that that's the way the suit went forth. I don't think the driver was mentioned. I never had any impression that he was; it was just against the company.

My instinct was that the car had broken down and that it was human error, whatever the circumstances. I just could not bring the suit against another person.

**Josh Chapin (Son):** That time was a little weird because my mom was still heartbroken that her partner wasn't alive anymore. She didn't want any money. She certainly found a way to do stuff with it, but after the settlement and after we were left a tremendous amount of money — and everybody knew it because it was in the newspaper — everybody wanted a piece of it. Everybody. Family members. Anybody my dad worked with.

(Harry) liked sycophants. He liked people who were going to tell him how amazing he was and he didn't have any quality control. If anybody took him seriously, he was going to take them seriously.

It was nasty. It was like it just had a nasty feeling about it. We've all benefitted tremendously from the work that was done. But yeah, it was stressful.

My mom still hates herself to this day for even letting (the lawsuit) happen because she didn't want to be part of it.

❉ ❉ ❉

**Ken Kragen (Second manager):** I have nothing but great memories of Harry. When I did "We Are the World," I always attributed much of doing that to Harry and felt at times, 'Gee, I wish Harry was here. He would have really led this activity. He would have really been the one to make things happen.'

On the other hand there was also a general feeling that maybe if he had been there he would have overwhelmed a lot of the artists that were there and maybe people wouldn't have participated.

**Jackson Browne (Musician):** I was moved by the way (Ken Kragen) honored him. It made (Harry's) memory last and helped his ideals to endure.

**Ken Kragen:** The freakiest thing about "We Are the World" was a Harry Chapin moment in many ways because I had gone to New York to look at the big spread that we were going to get in *Life* magazine. They did a big cover story and almost like an eight-page spread with photos. *Life* at that time was still very, very viable. I was being driven away in a car that I owned. I owned an old-fashioned limo from the '30s, I guess, or early-'40s. I had this car in New York, was being driven to the next appointment, and I had this weird feeling literally that Harry Chapin had crawled up inside of me and was orchestrating everything that I was doing. I'm not the most spiritual guy in the world but it was a very, very wild kind of experience to suddenly have that kind of thing happen. I sort of felt like, 'Oh my gosh. Harry's running the show here even if he's not alive!' [Harry] Belafonte often referred to him as one of our main inspirations in everything we did there.

※ ※ ※

**Charles Sanders (Friend; Producer, *1987 Carnegie Hall Tribute to Harry Chapin*):** I produced the (1987 Carnegie Hall tribute) show and the idea was, from a historical perspective, to cement Harry's place in American music history and have him be in the same league as the Woody Guthries [and] Pete Seegers, and have a document that would allow people to look back and see testimony from folks like Bruce Springsteen saying, 'This guy made a difference to me.' So that was the driving force behind putting the show together and doing it at Carnegie Hall.

**Jason Chapin (Son):** At the time, I was living in an apartment above my mother's office. So I was finding out on a day-to-day basis all the things that were happening leading up to the tribute. I think that was a very difficult time for my mother because Ken Kragen was going to produce it and then he had to back out.

Charlie Sanders, a good family friend, stepped in and did a wonderful job. But it was just very stressful because there were a lot of contract snags and people pulling out; and not knowing who was going to commit and come as far as the performers; and coordinating all the logistics with the Congressional Medal. Then I remember when Bruce Springsteen agreed to come and perform. That just made it a huge event.

**Sandy Chapin:** I realize that as a family, we have worked so hard to keep up the work that he had started and this involved the Carnegie Hall tribute. That was kind of an interesting experience too because Harry's friends in Congress had put forth his name for the Medal of Freedom. It was under [Ronald] Reagan, and Reagan turned it down. So then Congress came up with the Congressional Gold Medal — that would have been awarded to a small group of like close family; maybe he would get to invite 10 or 12 people or something to the White House, presented by Reagan. I said, 'Uh-uh.'

So we arranged through Pat Leahy that the Congressional Gold Medal could leave the White House and we could do this big tribute to Harry at Carnegie Hall because that's what he was: big crowds; big audiences; the cheap seats; and grassroots. We sent out 25,000 invitations all over the world because he had huge mailing lists. There was a lot of time and effort, and actually expense, on keeping WHY together, and Long Island Cares, and the Long Island Philharmonic — the things that (Harry) had started that were so important to him.

**Byron Dorgan (Friend; Former U.S. senator):** I offered a bill in the House striking a [Congressional] Gold Medal for Harry Chapin and got that passed. Then it got passed through the Senate. I did that because I thought the example that the late Harry Chapin had provided was such an extraordinary example that you could be an entertainer, you could have a public life, but you could also use your recognition and so on to make a big difference on something that matters to you.

I don't think anybody had more of an impact on the issue on trying to mobilize the fight against world hunger than Harry Chapin did. And he wasn't a politician.

**Patrick Leahy (Friend; U.S. senator):** I brought the Gold Medal up from Washington. Usually that's handed over either at the Capitol or at the White House. They didn't want it handed over at the White House because the Reagan administration cut back on hunger issues. So I took this Gold Medal; put it in a box; I put it in my briefcase; and I flew up to New York for Carnegie Hall. I held onto that briefcase — you'd think it was the nuclear codes. I did not want to set it down for a nanosecond. I was never so nervous in my life carrying something.

**Sandy Chapin:** Ken Kragen was going to be the producer. (Charlie Sanders) started putting ideas together and talking to people and was working with Ken Kragen. At one point Ken came to New York, invited me out to dinner, and said, 'I have to tell you something. I can no longer be the producer. I have gotten too involved in too many projects that have got me tied up in L.A.' Charlie was there too — it was Charlie, Ken Kragen, and myself. So Charlie, he was left holding the bag and this was not at a point where we could cancel. There were too many things lined up and invitations out. (Carnegie) Hall was booked. It was a very complicated thing.

I mean it's just incredible that (Charlie) could somehow survive through this whole thing because there were people hired, and then people quit, and then there were union problems, and then there were date problems. Basically, I would go to meetings in the city maybe about once a week, but mostly what I was doing was working a huge invitation list in Harry's office in Huntington because we wanted it to be representative. We wanted it to be like the Harry Chapin concert — which it certainly was because it was four-and-a-half hours long. It represented a lot of aspects of his life because it represented his work with the arts on Long Island and friends.... It was a really amazing cross section of people and supporters.

I think it was a fantastic evening for everybody, but there were so many glitches. The stage manager quit just before the concert and I think there was supposed to be a writer for a script and that fell out. And then Harry Belafonte, who was the emcee, was back there not getting any instructions from anyone; having to kind of make it up as he went along. Then the video didn't work. There were a lot of interesting glitches, but it was a great tribute.

**Charles Sanders:** It was a wide cross section of performers who talked about Harry's energy in trying to be a songwriter, and trying to be a performer, and trying to be a social leader, and an altruist, and how he had made an impression on his peers. Graham Nash; Judy Collins; Richie Havens; Pete Seeger; the Hooters came up from Philadelphia — they were a new band breaking on the scene. They wanted to talk about how they had been inspired and that there would be another generation of songwriters and performers who were influenced by Harry.

**Eric Bazilian (Musician, The Hooters):** We were offered "One Light [in a Dark Valley]." I clearly remember being on the tour bus and landing on the arrangement for the song.

**Charles Sanders:** The evening was more about peer recognition and establishing that tiny window that we had to work in ... before Harry's memory faded of getting people on the record to say, 'This guy lived.' I felt that was something I wanted to do. I think it was something Sandy wanted to do and we had an interesting time working together on it. I like to think it was one of the building blocks of keeping WhyHunger as a viable organization for all the years that followed.

## HARRY CHAPIN TRIBUTE

**Byron Dorgan:** Carnegie Hall was packed. It was an unbelievable cast of performers all performing obviously for nothing and donating their time. Bruce Springsteen, The Smothers Brothers, Pat Benatar, Graham Nash — the list goes on. Harry Belafonte. It was really extraordinary standing backstage waiting to go on the stage, standing next to Bruce Springsteen and all these people who had been involved in the life of Harry Chapin; and all of them who had been inspired by the energy of Harry Chapin.

**Terri Klausner (Performing artist):** It was one of the most fun, incredible evenings of my career. Tom had called me on the phone and said, 'Hey Terri, we're going to have the honor of being able to perform at Carnegie Hall to do a tribute to Harry and he's receiving a Congressional Medal of Honor for all of his work.' Tom said, 'We would love for you to be able to participate with us if you're available.' I was like, 'I'm available.'

I was seven-and-a-half months pregnant at the time. Tom goes, 'We have so many stars that we're doing a lot of the music, but would you sing "Tangled Up Puppet?"' And I was like, 'Absolutely. I'd be honored and thrilled.'

There we were in the dressing room at one point and Graham Nash came over and just started talking to us and he was as delightful and charming as he could possibly be. I could barely talk. It was just amazing. Then Bruce Springsteen came by. What's fascinating during that time too was that Bruce came out and mingled a little bit, but I never saw him stop writing. He was writing the whole time and I kept thinking to myself, 'Gosh, is he writing the song right now that he is going to perform or is he writing what he is going to say?' He had just small pieces of paper and his guitar with him.... Just writing the whole time.

Most of us, we would spill into the wings if we could. I just hung out in the wings and watched what was going on; watched the performers because I wanted to be there in the audience too. It was just really a thrill. It was beautiful to hear how everyone spoke of Harry. It was just amazing to be there and just be a part of it and see how much his music had influenced all these people. It was spectacular. It was a thrilling, thrilling, beautiful evening. I'm thrilled I just had an opportunity to rub elbows and just be there.

**Jason Chapin:** There were some great surprises, like when Graham Nash surprised my mother and sang "Sandy." Then my brother Josh putting the medal on the stool, which was representing how my father wasn't there but it was for him.

**Josh Chapin:** I remember being really scared of tripping. But other than that I had a girl I liked in the audience, so I was probably thinking about that.

**Jason Chapin:** Carnegie Hall was full and so there were so many fans there that had a chance to be part of that. All the artists from Pat Benatar, Paul Simon, and his brothers Tom and Steve, and Pete Seeger — it was just a wonderful collection of friends and fellow performers who were there. They all did tributes for other people, but it was just a special plus that it was our father's tribute and so many people had agreed to be a part of it.

**Eric Bazilian:** The atmosphere was amazing, bustling about hither and thither. All those legends just hanging out, waiting to perform on that stage. Everyone was warm, friendly. I remember having great conversations with Pete Seeger, Peter Yarrow, Pat Benatar.

**Tom Chapin (Brother):** I called Judy Collins and I said,

'What song do you want to do?' She says, 'Well, who's doing "Cat's in the Cradle?"' I said, 'Nobody.' She said, 'I'll do that.' I said, 'Well, Judy, it's great, but it's from a guy's point of view.' 'No it's not; it's from any parent's, about any kid.' I said, 'Bingo.' So she did it. She's done it ever since.

**Marie "Peachie" Marsden (Friend):** Paul Simon—they say he used to go out and do soup kitchens and stuff incognito. He'd dress up different. He didn't want to be known for doing it; he just did it.

Paul Simon came in late and said, 'Steve, I'd like to honor your brother. I always loved what he did.' Steve says, 'Well it's too late for the program.' (Simon) says, 'I don't want to be on the program. It doesn't matter.'

Harry Belafonte was the emcee and when he walked in he looked at ... the list, and he said, 'He's here? He's singing? Wow!' He was impressed with the people that were coming forward to sing Harry's music.

**Tom Chapin:** These things are more for the living than the dead. I mean it was an amazing night and it was worthwhile. My side of the thing was that Sandy really did all the heavy lifting on it and then suddenly realized she was over her head, and about a week or a week-and-a-half before the event called Steve and me and said, 'Help,' because nobody had talked about the specifics of it, you know. So we kind of jumped in in the end, which we were perfectly equipped to do. I mean it was an amazing night. For the people who were involved in it, it was a really emotional, transcendent night.

Springsteen was brilliant. He always is, right? But he was

brilliant that night articulating why we were there. But what's come full circle is the fact that it's 45 years of great work in the hunger issue. That's much more important, as far as I'm concerned.

In terms of Harry's legacy — Holy Christ, you know. The Gershwins, and [George M.] Cohan, and Irving Berlin have won the same award that Harry won. That's great company. But what Harry's done is pretty unique, you know. It's kind of in the world of Roberto Clemente — people who transcend what they do. They use who they are to move it into some other way of helping humanity. I mean that's pretty spectacular.

**Josh Chapin:** To me, when I think on that tribute I see my mom being stressed but actually really impressive. And it makes me love her even more because she really poured her heart and soul into things when she really wanted to go away and not be the keeper of the flame a lot. She loved the man so much and believed in so much of what he was doing, and just missed him.

❊ ❊ ❊

## I WONDER WHAT WOULD HAPPEN TO THIS WORLD

**Bill Ayres (Friend; Co-founder, WhyHunger):** You talk about some wonderful moments; the wonderful moments for the most part are that over the years, people have come into our world with talent, with money, with other resources, with connections and have just been wonderful to [WhyHunger]. There's no way we would have made it without those connections. Harry had made a lot of those connections. I made some too, but he had a lot of those connections. People didn't give up on us. I mean everybody thought that the organization would just go down the drain after he died, but we said, 'No.' None of the hunger organizations that we started went down the drain.

There are a number of younger people who grew up because their parents loved Harry. There's a whole generation of people who never saw him and most have never heard of him. But it's interesting that there are still a number of younger people who have been turned on by their parents. He created this whole genre of music called story songs, which is pretty interesting.

**Don Ruthig (Personal assistant):** There were times when you'd just get so wrought out and frustrated ... and you'd say, 'What the hell am I doing this for?' And then you listen to his music and, I think to some extent, that's still the reaction: 'You know what, it was his music more than anything to me.' I understand the man and all of his charitable things, but where he related to most people was through his lyrics and through his concert work. When I think back on him, that's what I remember.

**Josh Chapin:** (The Harry Chapin Foundation) was money that was taken from the settlement and we put aside. So from that, three or four times a year we make grants. It's a small organization comparatively to some of the larger ones, but I mean we usually give away about $75,000 to generally arts and education; community programs that are trying to feed people. It's usually about self-sufficiency and small organizations that are making big differences in their communities and that kind of carrying the mantle of what my dad believed in.

**Frances Moore Lappé (Friend; World hunger author):** Bono, I guess, is the new Harry but it was, at that time, really — and still is really — unusual for a popular singer to be so identified with social causes. Harry was the original.

✻ ✻ ✻

**Jen Chapin (Daughter):** The weird thing would be in this family if you decided you were going to be a stockbroker or a doctor even. But there was no pressure to do a responsible career. So I would say it was as much my uncles because I didn't connect directly with my father. What I really see is his legacy to me as an activist more than as a musician. I think I got my musical values from the wider family.

I often say if my dad were alive, I probably wouldn't be a musician because he would be so oppressively supportive that I wouldn't be able to deal with it.

**Jono Chapin (Son):** It's going to be different for different people. For some people, it's all going to be about the music. For other people, it's going to be about the activism. For others, there's specifics of poetry or what he meant to this cause or that cause. So inevitably I think that's the case because I think there were so many facets. The ability to know more about Harry is there and I think, in a lot of ways, that's maybe the fun of it is to bring that out.

At the same time I think the lesson is probably that we

all have talents; we just have to kind of find how to bring them to the fore and that's an ongoing process. Some people emerge to be feckless artists and they didn't pick up a paintbrush until their 70s. So it's just an ongoing process. Some of us are blessed with having a certain magnetism that is there earlier on and can latch on to it and have modes of expression, where others may be different. I think the message is reach inside and be willing to explore not only what each person has to offer, but what you can do together.

**Nancy Heller (Friend):** Harry would not care one bit about whether they name a road for him; whether he gets in the Rock & Roll Hall of Fame; whether they make a stamp for him. For him, what would be important was to know that people were still caring about his music and his causes and trying to make the world a better place. He believed that it takes all of us to make the world a better place. We all have a responsibility to help make it a better place. He was sort of the spokesman for doing that.

**Howard Fields (Drummer):** We try to tell his story too with the concerts we do. We don't just play the music. We tell little anecdotes and give a sense of what it was like to play music with him, to record music with him — just to be around him in general.

That's what's paying the bills on those shows. Harry's fans come and they see his band and his family and we're doing the songs that they love. So that's what they are all about.

**Sandy Chapin:** I will always miss the dialogue that we had because I've never had that experience since Harry died of just constantly filling up on questions. Both of us were very interested in trying to figure out what was kind of history of the moment.

**Big John Wallace (Bassist):** His legacy, to me, comes right down to the fact that everybody can make a difference. I mean one person can make a difference and I think that's what his life shows. Here's one guy that decided he wanted to make a difference in the hunger situation. He really did think it was an obscenity that in the richest country on Earth, 20 million people were going to bed hungry.... He knew that one person could make a difference, and instead of crying about things and bitching about things and doing nothing; it was get off your ass, get out there, and do something.

That's how he lived his whole life.

Holy shit!

# AUTHOR'S NOTE ON SOURCES

This oral biography is the result of more than 70 on-the-record interviews with those who knew Harry Chapin best — friends, family members, colleagues, and political and musical contemporaries included.

Any source incorporated into this book that has not been interviewed personally by the author — including Harry Chapin himself — is distinguished in *italicized* form throughout.

Sources, in alphabetical order, include:

**Howard Albert** – Co-producer, *Sequel* (November 10, 2020)

**Ron Albert** – Co-producer, *Sequel* (November 10, 2020)

**Eric Andersen** – Musician (December 15, 2020)

**Bill Ayres** – Friend; Co-founder, WhyHunger (August 24, 2010 and June 9, 2011)

**George Ball** – Cast member, *Jacques Brel is Alive and Well and Living in Paris* (February 21, 2012)

**Eric Bazilian** – Musician, The Hooters (January 27, 2012)

**Gerry Beckley** – Musician, America (September 27, 2019)

**Alexandra Borrie** – Cast member, *The Night That Made America Famous* (May 9, 2011)

**Oscar Brand** – Musician (May 31, 2011)

**Jackson Browne** – Musician (April 26, 2012)

**Diana Chapin** – Sister-in-law (November 29, 2010)

**Jason Chapin** – Son (December 14, 2010)

**Jen Chapin** – Daughter (September 23, 2010 and June 11, 2011)

**Jim Chapin** – Nephew (November 30, 2010)

**Jono Chapin** – Son (February 17, 2011)

**Josh Chapin** – Son (March 31, 2011)

**Sandy Chapin** – Wife (December 4, 2010)

**Tom Chapin** – Brother (February 5, 2011)

**Glenn Coleman** – Cadet, United States Air Force Academy Class of 1964 (July 12, 2011)

**Ingrid Croce** – Wife of musician Jim Croce (January 4, 2012)

**Anthony Curto** – Attorney (August 18, 2010)

**John Davidson** – Actor; Entertainer (September 5, 2011)

**Byron Dorgan** – Friend; Former U.S. senator (D-North Dakota) (September 28, 2011)

**Thomas Downey** – Friend; Former U.S. representative (New York 2nd Congressional District) (October 4, 2011)

**Mercedes Ellington** – Cast member, *The Night That Made America Famous* (May 13, 2011)

**Walter Falcon** – Member, Presidential Commission on World Hunger (March 28, 2014)

**Howard Fields** – Drummer (August 2, 2010 and August 17, 2010)

**Rex Fowler** – Musician, Aztec Two-Step (December 28, 2011)

**Stefan Grossman** – Musician (December 8, 2011)

**John Hall** – Musician, Orleans (May 17, 2019)

**Elspeth Hart** – Mother (September 23, 2010)

**Bob Heimall** – Former art director, Elektra Records (August 14, 2010)

**Nancy Heller** – Friend (March 25, 2011)

**Gary Howe** – Vice president, United States Air Force Academy Association of Graduates (May 4, 2011)

**Janis Ian** – Musician (December 27, 2011)

**Tommie Lee Jackson** – Backing vocalist, *Short Stories* (January 18, 2015)

**Chris Jacobsen** – Funeral director, A.L. Jacobsen Funeral Home, Huntington Station, N.Y. (October 6, 2011)

**Fred Kewley** – First manager (August 19, 2010)

**Terri Klausner** – Performing artist (March 15, 2014)

**Ken Kragen** – Second manager (August 10, 2010)

**Frances Moore Lappé** – Friend; World hunger author (October 20, 2010)

**Paul Layton** – Musician, The New Seekers (May 13, 2011)

**Patrick Leahy** – Friend; U.S. senator (D-Vermont) (December 14, 2020)

**Gordon Lightfoot** – Musician (February 8, 2011)

**James Maas** – Former professor, Cornell University (October 20, 2012)

**Marie "Peachie" Marsden** – Friend (December 11, 2010 and December 12, 2010)

**Melanie Marsden** – Friend (December 11, 2010 and December 12, 2010)

**Dave Marsh** – Friend; Music critic (February 21, 2011)

**David Miller** – Friend (March 26, 2011)

**Jaime Chapin Miller** – Daughter (July 24, 2011)

**Robert Mrazek** – Friend; Former U.S. representative (New York 3rd Congressional District) (October 3, 2011)

**Dave Neal** – Cadet, United States Air Force Academy Class of 1964 (May 9, 2011)

**John Oates** – Musician, Hall & Oates (January 30, 2015)

**Ron Palmer** – First guitarist (July 13, 2011)

**Allan Pepper** – Co-owner, The Bottom Line (January 7, 2012)

**Godfrey Pflager** – Editor, *Legendary Champions* (September 18, 2011)

**Zizi Roberts** – Friend; Backing vocalist, *Verities & Balderdash* (January 19, 2015)

**Don Ruthig** – Personal assistant (September 14, 2010)

**Charles Sanders** – Friend; Producer, *1987 Carnegie Hall Tribute to Harry Chapin* (December 2, 2010)

**Shelly Schultz** – Booking agent (February 24, 2011)

**Tim Scott** – First cellist (August 3, 2010)

**Niles Siegel** – Former album promotion man, Elektra Records (September 4, 2010)

**Stanley Snadowsky** – Co-owner, The Bottom Line (January 9, 2012)

**David Soul** – Actor; Musician (April 9, 2013)

**Joseph Stern** – Producer, *Chapin*; Conceiver, *Lies & Legends: The Musical Stories of Harry Chapin* (February 23, 2012)

**Livingston Taylor** – Musician (February 17, 2011)

**Martin Tubridy** – Inspiration for "Mr. Tanner" (July 14, 2019)

**Big John Wallace** – Bassist (July 9, 2011)

**Bob Zachary** – Former producer, Elektra Records (September 13, 2010)

✻ ✻ ✻

Cover and book photos provided courtesy of Chapin Productions LLC and *HarryChapinMusic.com*

# BIBLIOGRAPHY

Barnes, Clive. "Harry Chapin Brings Songs to Stage." *The New York Times*. 27 Feb. 1975, 30.

Belkin, Lisa, & Finder, Alan. "A Stunned Audience At the Park." *Newsday*. 17 July 1981.

Chapin, Harry. "A Couple of My Dreams For Long Island" (Special Reprint). *Newsday*. 1981, 9R, 10R.

Chapin, Harry. "All My Life's a Circle" (Concert program). *HarryChapin.com*, http://harrychapin.com/articles/bio.shtml. Accessed 9 Aug. 2010.

Chapin, Harry. "Unedited Typing Exercise." New York, 26 Feb. 1964.

Chapin, Sandy. "Harry Chapin Tribute" (Event program). New York, 7 Dec. 1987.

Gerson, Ben. "Records – Harry Chapin: *Heads & Tales*." *Rolling Stone*. 25 May 1972.

Holden, Stephen. "Review – *Sniper and Other Love Songs*." *Rolling Stone*. 7 Dec. 1972.

Holzman, Jac. "Taxi" (Original Promotional Video). *Elektra Records*. 1972.

Hughes, Allen. "Tubridy, a Bass-Baritone, Performs in 2d Recital Here." *The New York Times*. 17 Feb. 1972, 32.

Jahn, Mike. "Harry Chapin Sings Gorgeous Ballads." *The New York Times*. 24 July 1971, 16.

Marsh, Dave. "Singing for the World's Supper." *Rolling Stone*. 6 Apr. 1978.

*The Tonight Show Starring Johnny Carson*, NBC. Burbank, CA. 9 Sept. 1975. Television.

*The Tonight Show Starring Johnny Carson*, NBC. Burbank, CA. 10 Aug. 1977. Television.

Van Haintze, Bill, & Moreno, Sylvia. "Singer-Activist Harry Chapin Killed by Fiery Collision on LIE." *Newsday*. 17 July 1981.

# ACKNOWLEDGEMENTS

In addition to all sources interviewed, I would like to thank the many fans of Harry Chapin I've gotten to meet and interact with over the past 10 years for their support and encouragement. This includes David Ippolito, whose rendition of "What Made America Famous?" inspired me to write this book in the first place.

At the same time, I thank Harry Chapin for his strong influence over my life and work during this same time period.

This book was further made possible by several individuals who believed in it from the get-go and helped me see it through to completion. They include Shweta Agarwal, Dan Ankeles, Suzanne Cadgène, Brit DeLong, Patrick Emond, Judith Goetz, Lisa Larson, Steve Major, Tom Mashberg, Shawn Perry, Joseph Petrolawicz, Michael Sesling, Noreen Springstead, Pegge Strella, Laurel Sweet, Dick Wade, Mitchell Zuckoff; my family: Paul Kantor, Sandy Kantor, Samantha Kantor, Matilde Kantor, Patrick Close, Diane Close, Sean Close, Jessica Close; and, especially, my wife, Jen, and son, Freddie. With love and gratitude to you all!

In memory of Ethel Nelson. Give yourself a hug, Grandma!

## ABOUT THE AUTHOR

**Ira Kantor**

Ira Kantor is the creator of "Ira Kantor's Vinyl Confessions," a monthly music column for VintageRock.com. His writing has also appeared in the Boston Herald, Elmore Magazine, New York Daily News, and Village Voice. Ira resides outside Boston, Massachusetts with his wife, Jen, son, Freddie, and dog, Chapin. This is his first book.

Printed in Great Britain
by Amazon